SCHOOLBOY

Jim Tugerson: Ace of the '53 Smokies

By R. S. Allen

Copyright © 2008 by R. S. Allen

ISBN 0-7414-4986-2

Published by:

INFI∞ITY
PUBLISHING.COM

1094 New DeHaven Street, Suite 100
West Conshohocken, PA 19428-2713
Info@buybooksontheweb.com
www.buybooksontheweb.com
Toll-free (877) BUY BOOK
Local Phone (610) 941-9999
Fax (610) 941-9959

Printed in the United States of America

Printed on Recycled Paper

Published September 2008

Dedicated to

The Tugerson Family and Their Patriarch, Jim Tugerson

The 1953 Knoxville Smokies

And to Old Ballplayers Everywhere

Table of Contents

Acknowledgments

Grateful acknowledgement is given to the Tugerson family for the cover photographs and all other photographs contained herein that include Jim Tugerson, except the Bathers photograph, photographs given to or procured by Jim Tugerson during his baseball career.

Grateful acknowledgement is given to Ken Buckles for the photograph of Whitey Diehl and him in their Cincinnati uniforms taken in 1953.

Grateful acknowledgement is also given to David Clapp for the personal photograph of himself taken in 1958.

Grateful acknowledgements are given to the *Hot Springs Sentinel-Record* for permission to reprint the photograph of Jim and Leander Tugerson in their Bathers uniforms taken in April 1953, and to *The Herald* (Rock Hill, SC) for permission to reprint the photograph of David Mobley taken August 26, 1952.

Grateful acknowledgement is given to the Winter Haven Police Department for the departmental photo-graph taken in 1962.

Lastly, grateful acknowledgements are given to Ginger Wright for her photographs taken at the tribute on July 11, 2008 and to the Smokies for capturing the ceremonial first pitch.

Foreword

My first contact with the author (Bob Allen) was less than a month before a planned tribute for the late Jim Tugerson in Sevierville, Tennessee, the present home of the Tennessee Smokies, a Chicago Cubs affiliate. I was Jim's (I called him Tug) teammate on the 1955 Dallas Eagles of the then Texas League, and I agreed to write a letter to be read at that tribute. Tugerson had a very positive influence on me and my career that year in Dallas. I had resisted the Giant organization when they assigned me to Dallas. I was the only black player in the Carolina League in 1953 and did not want to experience overt racism again in the South.

I reluctantly agreed to go to Dallas and the club rented rooms for us in a private home. We also roomed together when the team was on the road. Tugerson was one of the reasons I had a successful playing career. He taught me to focus on the game, and to ignore the demented racist insults of bigoted fans in places like Shreveport and Beaumont. The next year Jim returned to pitch in Dallas. I was promoted to Minneapolis by the Giants.

After reading snippets from Bob Allen's proposed book, I agreed to write this foreword in honor of Tugerson and all the other great black players who never got the opportunity to play in the majors. I was always amazed how Tugerson never seemed bitter or resentful. His story, like others who suffered during segregation, needed to be told. Tugerson and others dealt with idiotic racial insults, segregation, lower pay, quotas, yet kept their dignity.

I visited Jim and his family after he retired. He was an officer in the Winter Haven, Florida Police Department for many years, rising to the rank of lieutenant. He died a family man, a respected community leader and a pioneer who helped me and many others become successful on and off the diamond. Jim Tugerson was my friend.

Bill White

National League President (1989-1994)

Introduction

This is the story of Jim Tugerson, a black baseball player, a pitcher, from Florence Villa, Florida, who in 1953 showed the baseball world and his Knoxville Smokies' teammates a side of him no one would ever forget, a side that defined him as a ball player and as a man. Although the focus of the story is Tugerson, it is by necessity also the story of the 1953 Knoxville Smokies. While Big Jim to his Knoxville teammates and fans, he was called Schoolboy by his other teammates and fellow police officers.

Schoolboy came to the Smokies because he was black. The acceptance of Jackie Robinson as the first black ball player to play in a league outside the Negro leagues had not permeated all areas of our bigoted society in 1953. Schoolboy and his brother, Leander, had agreed to play for the Hot Springs Bathers of the Cotton States League, but the league, rather than allow a mixed race team to play on the same diamond, forced the Hot Springs club to send them to Knoxville.

After being denied a second time to pitch for Hot Springs, Schoolboy's attorney filed a $50,000 civil rights lawsuit against the Cotton States League and others. At Knoxville he compiled 29 regular season wins and 4 playoff wins, making him the winningest pitcher in organized baseball that year. He rose above those who had denied him his right of choice. He rose above the fans around Knoxville's league that he termed "the little people," people who made hateful, mean-hearted but yet fruitless attempts to belittle and degrade him. He rose above the Knoxville press that disparaged his Smokies

1

team and teammates by uplifting the team with his talent and character, inspiring them to win the league championship and beating a team that had been consistently better all season. He rose above club ownership that allowed him to play in an outdated replacement uniform that embarrassed him even more when he had to wear it when barnstorming with Roy Campanella and other major league greats that had Dodgers, Indians, White Sox, and other such major league names sewn across their chests.

Schoolboy, whose contract with the Bathers was purchased by the Dallas minor league team, played another five years of minor league ball and never made it to the show. He returned to Florence Villa and had a 27-year law enforcement career with the Winter Haven Police Department, becoming a respected, effective, and influential leader on the force and in the community. But he never forgot baseball. Baseball never let him down. People did.

Chapter 1

The Opportunity

During the summer and fall of 1952, when I was 9 years old (I turned 9 in mid-August), my dad, at age 59, built a new restaurant in Sevierville, my small East Tennessee hometown. It was a business he had been in for over 20 years already only a block away, but he wanted to design the building, select the fixtures, and try out some new ideas he had been mulling around in his mind for no one knows how long. Except for a walk-up curb service window on the parking lot side of the building, the finished eatery looked remarkably like the building a block down the street.

Another change, however, a change that had nothing to do with design, concrete blocks, or mortar, favorably affected my life more than any other. The hiring of a full-time evening chef afforded my dad a much more flexible work schedule. I suspect he became accustomed to having the evenings free while building the new place. He had closed the old restaurant and only worked days during the new construction.

Besides giving my dad a challenge late in his business life and moving us further away from the annually flooding waters of the Little Pigeon River, this new business, accompanied by the increased flexibility, gave us the opportunity to do something there had never been time to do previously—go to an organized professional baseball game. This wasn't the only event, however, that granted us this perk.

The Knoxville Smokies had been around in total almost as long as my dad's beef stew lunch. Minor league baseball had come and gone from Knoxville a couple of times since 1925. The Smokies had played in three different leagues—the South Atlantic League (1925-1929), the Southern Association (1931-1944), and the Tri-State League (1946-1952). They had been affiliated with the Brooklyn Dodgers, the Pittsburgh Pirates, and the New York Giants.

The Smokies' ball park had always been just east of downtown Knoxville in a largely industrial area. The first park, utilized from 1925-1929, was called Caswell Park. It was torn down and was replaced in 1931 with the construction of a new park named Smithson Stadium.

In early 1953 the Knoxville City Council opted to tear down Smithson Stadium and build a new ball park. Although a number of sources indicate that Smithson Stadium burned to the ground, no evidence has been found to support this. In fact, the evidence indicates it was razed, not burned, and had been half demolished by April 1953. Tom Anderson, sportswriter for *The Knoxville Journal*, wrote in his column on April 2nd that city officials had received a letter the day before from the Baseball Hall of Fame in Cooperstown, N.Y. requesting planks from Smithson for display in the Hall. Demolition of Smithson was completed a couple of months later.

Jack Aragon, General Manager and part owner of the Smokies the previous three years pled with the City Council to postpone the demolition and construction until the fall, assuring the City Council he could field a team, but the decision was made to go ahead and build a new stadium. This action resulted in Knoxville losing its franchise in the Class B Tri-State League. It would be over a year before the Knoxville Municipal Stadium, renamed Bill Meyer Stadium in 1957, would be ready.

The 1953 Smokies played in a newly renovated and updated ball park built on Chapman Highway in Seymour, appropriately named Chapman Highway Park. *Few people now recall this park. Even fewer know that this was the first*

4

time the Smokies found a home in Sevier County, not in the year 2000 when they moved to Sevierville and became the Tennessee Smokies after Knoxville city officials declined to replace or update the dilapidated Bill Meyer Stadium.

This park location further enhanced my opportunity to experience professional baseball as Seymour was only 12 miles away, halfway between Sevierville and Knoxville. This was important because my dad would never, on a regular basis, have taken me to Knoxville for a baseball game.

In fairness to my dad, however, he knew how much I loved baseball. He knew because he saw the gloves, bats, and balls that accumulated at my birthday and at Christmas. He knew because of the baseball cards and bubble gum that came from Pete Emert's store a half block from Allen's Café. And he knew because of the window panes he had replaced in Doc Ingle's garage apartment two backyards away.

The ball park was perfect. There was a covered grandstand behind home plate. It was all wood, painted green. The fence was freshly painted with business ads familiar to me. The grass was very green, the infield immaculately manicured. It had all the sights, sounds, and smells of a minor league ball park. It was the best I had ever seen.

This team and this ball park came about through the efforts of one Byron Kitchens, the president of Knox Baseball, Inc. According to newspaper accounts, Kitchens and four other investors put up $2,500 each, a total of $12,500, the amount reportedly needed to incorporate and buy into the franchise. Kitchens was a newcomer to such an investment and relied heavily on his father, who had been involved with minor league baseball for a number of years in south Georgia.

Under baseball law at that time, Kitchens was on

good footing as anybody or group could take over "open territory." Kitchens and his investors were able to take over the territory vacated by Knoxville and the Mountain States League franchise vacated by the Hazard, Kentucky team, the league champions in 1952, after Hazard failed to post an entry fee. Kitchens was so intent on fielding a team in time for the April 25th opener that he even advertised for players in the April 8th issue of *The Sporting News*.

In 1953 the Smokies played in the Class D Mountain States League for the first and only time in its history and were managed by Vince Pankovits, a playing manager who was also the team's catcher. There were seven other teams from Tennessee, Virginia, and Kentucky in the league including the Maryville-Alcoa Twins, the Kingsport Cherokees, the Morristown Red Sox, the Norton Braves, the Big Stone Gap Rebels, the Harlan Smokies, and the Middlesboro Athletics. Neither this Smokies team nor its players were in any way affiliated with any major league team. Rather, this team was mostly comprised of rookies, but it had a few veterans, albeit with limited experience.

All of these teams were in close proximity to one of the Smokies' two "home bases"—Knoxville and Pennington Gap, Virginia. Knoxville and Seymour (location of Chapman Highway Park) were within 20 miles of Hunt Field, the home field of the Maryville-Alcoa Twins and 40 miles from Morristown. Kingsport was 85 miles from Knoxville but only 35 miles from Pennington Gap. The two Virginia teams—Big Stone Gap and Norton—were in close proximity to Pennington Gap, as was Harlan, Kentucky, only 20 miles away. The longest drive from Pennington Gap was to Middlesboro, Kentucky, located at the point where Kentucky, Tennessee, and Virginia connect, but it was just over 40 miles.

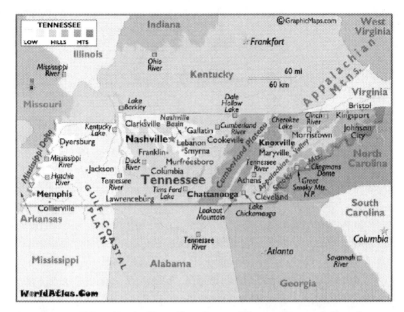

Tennessee Map Including Southeast Kentucky and Southwest Virginia

The Smokies opened the season at Alcoa against the Twins on Saturday, April 25th. They christened the new Chapman Highway Park the following day. *I know I didn't attend opening day as Sunday afternoons were always reserved for a visit to my maternal grandparents. I can't recall the number of games my dad and I attended, but we attended numerous times throughout the summer. I do recall, however, that I was not prepared for what I saw at several of those 1953 games at Chapman Highway Park.*

Chapter 2

The Eyes of a 9-Year-Old

"Big Jim" Tugerson was the most impressive athlete I had ever seen. He was 30 years old when he came to Knoxville, and was tall, lanky, and confident in his abilities. He seemed out of place because he was so much better than any of the other pitchers in the league. He had a sidearm delivery that seemed, because of his long arm, to extend almost to third base when he threw. Because of the velocity, his fastball was an automatic "cross-fire" that backed both right and left-handed hitters off the plate. At the end, the pitch would find the corner.

It really didn't matter that his fastball tailed the way it did. Very few hitters could touch it right down the pipe. I can recall wondering at the time that if the major league pitchers are better than him, how does any hitter in the major leagues ever get any wood on the ball?

Big Jim caused an excitement that summer for a lot of people. My dad and I always tried to go when he pitched, and the few times we went when he wasn't pitching, we were disappointed.

Jim had a younger brother, Leander, who came with him to the Smokies. Unfortunately, his stint was cut short due to a sore arm, and we never got to see him pitch. Leander had a record of 3 wins and 5 losses and an ERA of 5.55 when he returned home to Florida. [For those unfamiliar, ERA stands for Earned Run Average which is the mean of earned runs (scored by hits, not errors) given up by a pitcher per nine innings pitched.]

Both Jim and Leander had grown up playing baseball on county and semi-pro teams at their home, Florence Villa, Florida, both before and after their military stints. They had been instrumental in the Indianapolis Clowns winning championships in the Negro American League in 1951 and 1952, giving the historically entertainment-geared Clowns an air of newly found respectability. Both had initially signed contracts in 1953 to play for the Hot Springs Bathers of the Class C Cotton States League. This league consisted of teams in Arkansas, Mississippi, and Louisiana.

On April 20th, the day before the Bathers' opening game, the Tugersons were barred from playing because of their race by a vote of the other teams' owners and were optioned the same day to Knoxville. Jim was recalled by Hot Springs in mid-May after the Bathers' pitching staff and attendance had dwindled. On May 20th while warming up to pitch against the Jackson team, the league stepped in, thwarting his second effort to pitch, and forfeited the game to Jackson. Tugerson returned to Knoxville to finish the season.

By the end of May, Kitchens and his investors were reportedly $21,000 in debt after renovating the ball park, spending $8,000 for lights, buying uniforms and equipment, and paying salaries and expenses. Attendance was down and there was not even enough money to buy baseballs. On May 28th a game against Morristown had to be forfeited because the Smokies ran out of balls in the 7th inning.

On June 1, 1953, Dr. Edgar Grubb and other Knoxville investors bought the franchise for the remainder of the season. The first thing the new owners did was to set up and promote "Jim Tugerson Night" on June 5th. They arranged for low-cost bus transportation from east Knoxville, the city's predominantly black area, and free admission to all black fans. After the game, which Big Jim pitched and won, he received gifts of gratitude from several fans.

We attended this game. I remember because my dad's dishwasher, Osborne, and his brother, Marshall, went with us.

There weren't many black families in Sevierville but

9

*between my dad and mom, they knew all of them. Dad
always had two black employees to help him in the kitchen, a
cook and a dishwasher. He didn't like it, but he couldn't
afford to let the black customers eat in his restaurant. He
always had a table set up in the kitchen to accommodate the
black patrons, and there was always plenty of business in the
kitchen, especially on the weekends.*

*Osborne, accompanied by Marshall, had come to our
house once at midnight. Osborne had been jumped walking
home from work and badly beaten. They came to our house
because they had no where else to go for help. Marshall, the
size of an NFL offensive lineman, was so mad I know he
would have killed that night had he been able to put his
hands on those responsible. My mom patched up Osborne,
and he recovered. I heard some time later that Marshall had
broken a man's middle finger by bending it back on top of
his hand. I never knew for certain that it was the person
responsible for assaulting Osborne, but I always suspected
that it was.*

*Osborne worked in the restaurant for several years,
longer than anyone else who worked in the kitchen, and he
was my friend. Osborne was a deaf mute and taught me the
hand alphabet and to sign. He helped me build things out of
vegetable crates—a boat, an airplane, and the like. We'd
chalk a circle on the kitchen's concrete floor and shoot
marbles. We'd go outside before it got dark and throw a
baseball in the gravel parking lot. Osborne, who would
always tell me he was going to get fired if he didn't stop
playing and get back to work, also loved baseball.*

*Because I was 9 years old the summer of 1953, I
never equated Jim Tugerson pitching for the Smokies with
the black customers having to eat in my dad's kitchen. It
never occurred to me then that Big Jim might have had pain
inflicted on him because he, like Osborne, was black. I knew
there were black players in the major leagues because I
collected baseball cards. When I watched him pitch I simply*

saw a great baseball player that happened to be black. In retrospect I was glad I was 9 years old at that time.

The Smokies played 125 games in 1953 and ended with 70 wins and 55 losses. The Maryville-Alcoa Twins won the regular season, but the Smokies won the playoffs three games to one. Tugerson won 29 and lost 11 games. In addition, he won four games during the playoffs. He pitched 330 innings, struck out 286, and had an ERA of 3.71. He also recorded five shutouts. The Smokies' attendance exceeded 36,000 for the sixty or so home games that summer.

Probably the most recognized batter Tugerson faced in 1953 was 19-year-old Willie Kirkland, an outfielder who went on to have a 9-year major league career with the Giants and the Indians and later played six years in Japan. Kirkland had 164 RBIs for the Maryville-Alcoa Twins during the 1953 season.

The Smokies were back in Knoxville at the new Knoxville Municipal Stadium for the 1954 season. They were again members of the Class B Tri-State League, their last season to ever play in this league. Knoxville would be without baseball in 1955 but the Smokies returned in 1956 as members of the South Atlantic League.

Besides the Smokies, the 1954 Tri-State League included the Asheville Tourists, the Greenville Spinners, the Spartanburg Peaches, the Rock Hill Chiefs, and the Anderson Rebels. Again, the Smokies came in second in the regular season but defeated Asheville in the playoffs three games to one. The Smokies were good, the ball park was great, but the magic was gone. Big Jim was gone.

For some six years after seeing Jim Tugerson pitch during the summer of 1953, I attempted to emulate his style of pitching, and, in particular, his sidearm delivery. I never had his arm strength so I was unable to master his crossfire, but I did develop a respectable sidearm curve ball. After

11

Little League and Babe Ruth ball, there was little opportunity to play organized ball. Football was king at my high school, not baseball. Basketball was played by most to stay in shape for football.

My high school had a baseball team only once in my four years, in 1959. We played one game against a neighboring county high school, and I got the call as our starting pitcher. Our manager was the defensive line coach, the biology teacher, and the chemistry teacher. The field where we played had shoulder-high roofed sheds that served as dugouts, but they were not dug out. Each time I got into trouble, our manager, a short, stocky man of muscular build, would rise to come to the mound. Each time he did so, however, he hit his head on the dugout framing and then would stagger back to the bench holding his head. This happened two or three times during the course of the game, and each time I would get out of trouble and end the inning before he could recover. The last time he did this was in the last inning with bases loaded and two out. As he was staggering back for the last time, I fielded a come-backer and threw home for the force out. The game was over, and we had won four to two.

My only high school pitching performance didn't compare to any of the games I had seen Big Jim pitch, but it felt good to throw sidearm and end the season with a record of 1-0 and an ERA of 2.00.

Before the umpire yelled "Play ball!" at the opener for the Smokies at Hunt Field in Alcoa, there was obvious resentment that the Knoxville Smokies were based in Sevier County, not Knoxville, and that this had been brought about by five young entrepreneurs after the Knoxville City Council voted baseball out for the 1953 season. Knoxville had no minor league team inside its city limits, a fact which upset numerous factions: the fans, baseball investors, and baseball managers like former manager Jack Aragon, the City Council members who had opposed the demolition of

Smithson Park and the construction of the new Knoxville Municipal Stadium in early 1953, and a goodly number of sportswriters.

Before and after the season began, *The Journal* sarcastically referred to the team as the "Chapman Park Seviers," rather than the Knoxville Smokies. Sportswriter Ed Harris, in his April 29th column gave two reasons for the newspaper calling the club the Chapman Park Seviers. First, the team played in Chapman Park in Sevier County, and second, the Harlan club was also called the "Smokies," thus creating a confusing situation. Harris acknowledged the paper had received a letter from a Mountain States League official complaining. He jokingly closed the subject by offering a compromise "...when the Chapman Park entry wins we'll call them Seviers—when they lose we will call them Smokies '...The same old Smokies....' "

Tom Anderson noted in his May 7th column that the Smokies' owners could escape criticism for using the Smokies' name by changing the nickname to the "Dark Stars," a pluralized version of Dark Star, the long-shot that beat Kentucky Derby favorite Native Dancer. He opined that it would be appropriate since the Tugersons had proved to be the "mainstays of the roster."

The Journal called the Smokies team the Chapman Park Seviers or the Chapman Park Smokies until the Knoxville investors, who had been rebuffed by the Knoxville City Council in January, 1953, took over the franchise on June 1st. Only then did *The Journal* refer to the team as the Knoxville Smokies. *The Journal* did this even though the team continued to play at the Chapman Highway Park. *The Knoxville News-Sentinel,* the other Knoxville daily paper, had called them the Knoxville Smokies from the outset.

Chapter 3

The Wrangling

George Dempster and Cas Walker were bitter political enemies. Dempster, a Democrat, was born in Knoxville. Walker, a Republican, was born in neighboring Sevier County. Both were self-made successful businessmen with considerable political influence. Dempster invented and manufactured the Dempster Dumpster used for the collection and disposal of waste. Walker established a chain of supermarkets in East Tennessee that extended to Pennington Gap, Virginia. Both men resided in North Knoxville. And this is where the similarities ended.

Dempster was appointed Knoxville city manager in 1929, 1935, and 1945. He was an unsuccessful Republican candidate for Governor of Tennessee in 1940, losing by a substantial margin. He served on the Knoxville City Council from 1948 to 1949 and as Mayor from 1951 to 1955. The quote most frequently attributed to him about Walker was, "If I ordered a boxcar load of sons of bitches and they only sent me Cas, I'd pay for the whole order."

Cas Walker, who preferred the nickname "The Ole Coon Hunter," served on the Knoxville City Council from 1942 to 1971, except for one year—from the fall of 1946 to the fall of 1947. Walker, who had been elected Mayor by the Council in January, 1946, fired his appointed City Manager, Dempster, whom Walker viewed as the ring leader of the "Silk Stocking Crowd". As a result, there were cries for Walker's recall. Instead, he lost his seat on the Council for a year but easily won re-election.

Cas Walker was an icon of East Tennessee mountain culture. He left home at age fourteen to work at a North Carolina paper company and worked in Kentucky coal mines when he was in his twenties, saving enough to open his first grocery store in 1924. In the '50's he sponsored a musical variety show and a gospel singing show on local television, and pitched his groceries on both shows himself. The "Cas Walker Farm and Home Hour" helped launch the careers of the Everly Brothers and Dolly Parton. "Mulls Singing Convention," hosted by the Reverend J. Bazzel Mull, his neighbor, aired for decades. He prefaced most significant comments with "Well, neighbors, I'm a tellin' you." Walker gained national recognition in March, 1956 when a photograph of him taking a swing at another city councilman appeared in Life magazine. To this day there are still disagreements as to whether this incident was staged. Some viewed Cas Walker as a champion of the common man; others saw him as an embarrassment.

On January 27, 1953, with Dempster presiding as Mayor and Walker as one of the seven Council members, the subject on the agenda was baseball. Specifically, the question before the Council was whether to raze Smithson Stadium and begin construction of the new stadium right away or wait until baseball season was over to start the project. Over a year prior to the meeting, Knox County voters had approved a $500,000 bond issue to build the new stadium; however, the demolition of the old stadium had not begun, much less the construction of the new one. Members knew that the more time that passed, rising labor and materials costs, especially steel, would end up shrinking the stadium.

At an earlier meeting, the Council had voted to wait until September to start construction, but things had changed. The New York Giants, the Smokies' affiliate for the past three years, had pulled out of Knoxville. Mayor Dempster and an apparent majority of the City Council members favored going ahead with the new stadium while exploring other options. Dempster had spoken with a University of Tennessee athletic official about the possibility of using the Vols' baseball stadium, Hudson Field. Under this plan, UT would allow use not only by the Smokies, but also by the city's recreation leagues as well. Hudson Field, however, had one huge drawback. It had no lights.

Among those at the meeting in favor of waiting to build were Jack Aragon, who managed the Smokies in 1950 and 1951 and became general manager in 1952; James Burke, businessman and past Smokies' co-owner; State Senator E. B. Bowles; and interested baseball fans. Aragon was accompanied by his attorney, R. C. Smith, an elected member of the Council three years before.

Angel V. "Jack" Aragon was a baseball man to the core. Born in Havana, Cuba, his father was with the Yankees organization for about three years. Aragon first played as a catcher in 1937 with the Greenwood Giants of the Cotton States League. The following year he led the Northeast Arkansas League in RBIs while playing for the Blytheville Giants. In 1940, he played for the Fort Smith Giants in the Western Association. He went on to be a batting practice catcher for the New York Giants in 1941 and on August 13th he made his only major league appearance as a pinch runner. Aragon played baseball while serving with the United States Coast Guard at Ellis Island, New York 1942-1944. Upon discharge, he signed with the Minneapolis Millers of the American Association as a free agent. He played the next three years in the Boston Red Sox farm system with the Louisville Colonels when he was sold to the Giants to become player-manager at Fort Smith in the Cotton States League. In 1949, he managed Jacksonville in the South Atlantic League before taking over the Smokies. Aragon was indeed a baseball man to the core.

Aragon argued that if the Council elected to build and not have baseball in 1953, Knoxville ran the risk of losing baseball for good regardless of the stadium to be built. He assured the Council that he had sufficient financial backers to obtain a franchise in the Southern Association, and Smith indicated Aragon had been able to negotiate a franchise that week in the Tri-State League. Aragon informed the Council he already had a working agreement with the New York Yankees and the Cincinnati Reds organizations to furnish players. Aragon and Burke assured the Council that there was sufficient backing to support a franchise. At Bowles' suggestion, the Council agreed to postpone the decision concerning the stadium until their meeting scheduled for three days later on Friday, January 30th.

On Friday, the Council voted 5-to-1 to proceed with the plan to build the new stadium right away and not have organized professional baseball in Knoxville the 1953 season. Cas Walker, whose position opposing immediate construction was well known, was not present to vote. Aragon and his investors were asked to wait another year with the belief that the new stadium would bring even better baseball to Knoxville than had been played in the past. A heated exchange transpired when Bowles accused Dempster of trying to dictate to the Council on the stadium issue, stating, "It seems like you are trying to push this thing mighty hard." Bowles further stated, "It seems to me that these gentlemen are the elective body. They should be the ones to say." Dempster assured Bowles the Council couldn't be pushed "any more than I can be pushed. You can't push Dempster one inch, big boy," Bowles then asked, "Any other questions you want to ask me?" Dempster responded by saying, "I didn't want to ask you any in the first place." After Bowles left the meeting, Dempster, who viewed Bowles' effort as an insult, apologized for Bowles' actions.

Such political wrangling over baseball in Knoxville would resurface from time to time over the next half century. The wrangling would finally go away for good in 1999 and so would the Smokies. Again, it would boil down to a new stadium issue—not when it should be built, but rather if it should be built at all. Like 1953, Sevier County in 2000 would welcome the Smokies with open arms with the construction of a 19 million dollar stadium.

Chapter 4

The Early Years, the Rebuffs, and the Law Suit

Both of the Tugerson brothers played a lot of baseball before joining the Indianapolis Clowns. They grew up playing baseball in Florence Villa, the black community in Winter Haven, Florida. Both played in the Winter Haven city league for an all black team made up of Florence Villa residents. It was during his time in the city league that his teammates would tag Jim with the nickname "Schoolboy," likening him to Schoolboy Rowe, a nickname that stayed with him the rest of his life. Jim's daughter, Tina, who shared many wonderful stories about her dad with me, related that the other players thought her dad pitched like Rowe.

Lynwood Thomas "Schoolboy" Rowe, a white 6'4" Texan, got his nickname from his teammates while playing on a men's team when he was a 15-year-old boy still in school. A right-handed pitcher, Rowe played for the Detroit Tigers, the Brooklyn Dodgers, and the Philadelphia Phillies in a major league career that spanned the years between 1933 and 1949. He had a record of 158-101, recorded 913 strikeouts, and a career ERA of 3.87. Rowe was a power pitcher with great control, leading the American League in strikeout-to-walk ratio in 1934 and 1935. He also was an excellent hitting pitcher, batting over .300 in these two years and finished his career with 18 home runs and 153 RBIs. Rowe may be best remembered for a comment he made during the nationally broadcast Eddie Cantor radio show in September, 1934, when he said, "How'm I doing, Edna honey?" Edna was his fiancée whom he married following the 1934 World Series.

Schoolboy pitched for the Bartow All-Stars and had opportunities to pitch for the Kansas City Monarchs, the Indianapolis Clowns, and the Homestead Grays before finally joining the Clowns and his brother, Leander, in 1951. Jim had been content with life in Florence Villa where he was raising a family with his wife, Ora Lee. He was making $50 a game every week and was cooking at the Sundown Restaurant. He was making a good living for his family but the lure of organized baseball overtook him.

Leander and Jim Tugerson started their professional baseball career with the Indianapolis Clowns of the Negro American League; Leander, at age 23, in 1950, and Jim, at age 28, a year later. The Clowns had been a black touring team that mixed comedy with baseball in the same way the Harlem Globetrotters did in basketball. In fact, "Goose" Tatum played for both the Clowns and the Globetrotters. The Clowns, however, had toned down the entertainment in order to gain admittance into the league.

The Clowns were a good team and in 1951 with the Tugersons on the pitching staff posted a 53-26 record and won both the first and second half titles. Leander oddly enough at that time was the better pitcher and compiled a 15-4 mark which included an August no-hitter against the Birmingham Black Barons when he struck out 16. Jim had 10 wins and 5 losses in his first year of professional ball. Following the season Leander signed a contract with the Chicago White Sox, and although he was intended to have gone to the Sox' Colorado Springs club, he returned to the Clowns the following year.

In 1952 the Clowns went 26 and 18, and Jim accounted for 14 of those wins with only two losses. With the help of the Tugersons and an 18-year-old Hank Aaron, the Clowns won the first half. Although eleven years his senior, Tugerson roomed with Aaron during the time they both were with the Clowns. Their personalities were similar in that they practiced clean living—no drinking, no smoking, no chasing women. Tugerson, married with five children, and Aaron both had the same goal—to play baseball in the major leagues. Jim finished that season with Oriente of the Dominican Summer League while Aaron's contract was sold to the Boston Braves for $10,000.

Indianapolis Clowns 1952

L. to R., Jim, Leander, Manager Buster Haywood, and Ray Neil

In February 1953, H. M. Britt and Lewis Goltz, who owned a controlling interest in the Hot Springs Bathers of the Class C Cotton States League, a non-integrated circuit with three teams in Arkansas, one in Louisiana, and four in Mississippi, signed both Jim and Leander to contracts for the 1953 season. On April 1 Mississippi Attorney General J. P. Coleman proclaimed that it would violate "public policy" to allow whites and Negroes to compete on the same teams.

The following evening the Tugersons were unanimously endorsed by the Bathers' board of directors, saying they would be given a chance to make the team. Acting club President Goltz said, "We don't want to disorganize the league in any way by playing the Negros, but we think these boys deserve a chance."

Four days later on April 6th the league directors ousted the Hot Springs club for refusing to release the Tugersons because they had been barred from playing in Mississippi. The league officials, following a 3-hour closed meeting in Greenville, Mississippi, notified the Hot Springs club that the action was taken for the "survival of the league." Officials of the Hot Springs club said they would "fight to the finish" to regain its Cotton States League franchise without releasing the Tugersons. A. G. Crawford, president of the Bathers, said, "We are not taking it lying down. We don't interpret playing colored players on our club as being detrimental to any club."

On April 6th the following joint statement was issued by the Tugersons on their behalf by the Bathers:

"Are we fit to work in your homes and fields only? We can talk for you and help elect you when it is time for voting. When you were young was it fair for a Negro maid to raise you? Now we're the forgotten ones. You haven't been fair to us in the South. We don't want to, as Negroes, stay with you or eat with you. All we want to do is play baseball for a living...As long as the club wants us, we will stay here and fight."

Crawford called an open meeting of club directors and fans for April 7th to be followed by an executive session of the directors. Crawford said, "We hadn't anticipated this sort of reaction. We thought there might possibly be a little resentment and we offered to compromise and use the players only where they are welcome." In addition to the directors and fans, Crawford also invited Leslie M. O'Connor, a member of the executive committee of the National Baseball Association. O'Connor had called the move "the most grievous error ever committed in baseball." Crawford did not question the right of the league to expel clubs for "certain violations," but he did not consider signing Negro players a violation.

At the April 7th meeting the Bathers' board of directors petitioned the National Association of Minor Professional Leagues to reinstate the Hot Springs club in the Cotton States League. The board drew up a resolution protesting the removal of its franchise because of its refusal to dismiss the Tugersons. This action followed a statement by Jim Tugerson delivered in a shaky voice in which he offered to withdraw from the team in order "not to break up the Cotton States League. In the interest of the sport of baseball, I am asking that my contract and that of my brother, Leander, be assigned to a team in another league provided that the Hot Springs franchise is re-instated." Tugerson continued that Leander and he felt that the Hot Springs club "has gone to extremes in our support and we want to show our appreciation."

On April 11th, George M. Trautman, President of the National Baseball Association, ordered the Cotton States League to re-admit the Hot Springs club. Three days later, the league owners held another secret meeting and voted to re-admit the Bathers. Rumor had it that some sort of compromise regarding the Tugersons had been agreed upon, but the rumor remained unconfirmed as there was a $1,000 fine for disclosing details of the meeting. The next day Trautman deplored the action taken at the April 6th meeting, stating it was an illegal flouting of the league's constitution. He continued by saying that even if the procedures had been correctly followed, that if the only reason for banishment was "the employment of two Negro players, this office would still be required to declare the forfeiture invalid. The employment of Negro players has never been, nor is now, prohibited by any provision of the Major-Minor League Agreement."

Jim and Leander

Hot Springs Bathers April 1953

And then on April 20th, the day before the Bathers' opener, the Tugersons were abruptly optioned to the Knoxville Smokies of the Class D Mountain States League. The Bathers' Secretary, W. D. Rodenberry issued a statement saying the team didn't "want to embarrass the sport of baseball, the colored players or any other players or managers by giving the Tugerson brothers an opportunity to

prove their ability in the Cotton States League. He also referred to the April 7th statement of the Tugersons when they had asked to be transferred to another league if their presence meant the end of the Cotton States League. Even after the roller-coaster ride to this ending, Jim Tugerson said that Leander and he had no hard feelings and expressed hope that "some day we might be able to return."

Tugerson's words were almost prophetic. He would return twice during the 1953 season, neither time ending the way he would have liked. The first was in May, the second was in July.

On May 19th the Bathers, experiencing pitching and attendance problems, recalled Tugerson and scheduled him to pitch the following evening at home against the Jackson, Mississippi club. A crowd of 1,700 booed when plate umpire Thomas McDermott, accompanied by Hot Springs general manager Joe Thomas and Jackson manager Duke Doolittle, announced that he had been instructed by league president Al Haraway to forfeit the game to Jackson, 9-0, if Tugerson appeared in the line-up. Tugerson was taking his warm-up pitches when the game was forfeited. An Associated Press wire photo of Tugerson flanked by two white Hot Springs players on each side listening to the announcement appeared in *The Knoxville Journal* issue of May 23, 1953.

The day following the forfeiture Haraway explained his action by saying the Hot Springs club had violated a "gentlemen's agreement" entered into the previous month in which the Bathers agreed to dispose of the Tugersons in return for certain unnamed concessions. Haraway related, "The Hot Springs matter has cleared itself up." He opined that the matter was settled for good this time and canceled a league meeting he had previously scheduled. It was reported at the same time that Bathers' president Lewis Goltz, who led the fight for the Tugersons to pitch in the Cotton States League, had resigned and transferred his stock in the club. Tugerson was re-optioned back to Knoxville. Before leaving

Hot Springs, however, he reportedly consulted with attorneys about filing a civil rights suit against Haraway and the league.

An interesting side bar to these events is an Associated Press story out of Atlanta dated May 15th bearing the headline "**Negro Ball Players Accepted in Dixie**" in the May 17th issue of *The Knoxville News-Sentinel*, just two days prior to Tugerson being recalled to Hot Springs. The article included the now well-known photo of the Tugersons smiling in their Bathers uniforms with the following text: "THEY'RE ACCEPTED HERE"-- "Big Jim Tugerson, left, and brother Leander, who were optioned to Knoxville by the Cotton States League Hot Springs club, are freely accepted by the baseball fans at Chapman Highway Park where the Knoxville club plays its Mountain State League home games. What's more, they're the most effective hurlers on the club." The text of the story highlights the successes of integrated baseball teams in the South. The story recounted the events that brought the Tugersons to Knoxville while at the same time saying, "Every night in almost every state below the Mason-Dixon Line, you can find Negro and white players on the diamonds together." Apparently this sports writer did not check the ball parks in Georgia, Alabama, Mississippi, Louisiana, Arkansas, and Tennessee representing the Southern Association and the Cotton States League. Only one black player ever played in the old Southern Association. That player, Nat Peeples, played in two consecutive games for the Atlanta Crackers when the team opened in Mobile in April, 1954, but was demoted a week later to Jacksonville.

Following his 20th win in a game against Kingsport at home on the evening of July 13th Tugerson left town without telling anyone on the team, not even Pankovits, his manager, where he was going or why. The next day *The Journal* reported Tugerson had filed suit on July 13th at Hot Springs seeking $50,000 from the Cotton States League and quoted an unnamed "new source" that Tugerson went to Hot Springs upon the advice of his attorney. Smokies owner Dr. Edgar Grubb declined comment about Tugerson's whereabouts or plans but did say that Leander Tugerson had been advised not to pitch any more this season, had been placed on the injured list, and, in fact, had gone to his home in Florida.

The Hot Springs attorney who filed the suit on Tugerson's behalf was James Wood Chesnutt, a well respected civic leader and attorney with the firm of Wood, Chesnutt, & Smith. He was a 1938 graduate of Princeton University and a 1947 graduate of the University of Arkansas School of Law. He later served as an elected chancery court judge for over 20 years.

In the suit, filed in the U. S. District Court for the Western District of Arkansas, Hot Springs Division, Tugerson named as defendants the Cotton States League; Al Haraway, individually and as league president; all eight clubs in the league; and four officials of the teams in Mississippi, contending that the 14th Amendment to the U. S. Constitution, guaranteeing equal rights to all citizens, had been violated by the league when he was barred from playing after signing with the Bathers. In addition to cash damages, the suit sought a court order forcing the league to let him play.

Tugerson returned to Knoxville on July 17th and pitched the following night at Kingsport. The comments attributed to him that followed him home from Hot Springs indicated that he had given up the fight to play at Hot Springs "for this season." He also allegedly related that trying to play at Hot Springs would be a "waste of time to me, it would hurt my record." Henry Britt, the Bathers attorney, said Tugerson was returned to Knoxville to avoid having him suspended "if he plays with the Hot Springs baseball club." The feeling among his Smokies teammates was that he got some bad advice from someone in filing the lawsuit.

In the second week of September, U. S. District

Judge John Miller, Hot Springs, dismissed the civil rights portion of the Tugerson's lawsuit, opining that only the government could violate an individual's civil rights, not a corporate entity such as the Cotton States League or its representatives. Judge Miller held judgment on the breach of contract claim in abeyance, but before he could render a judgment, a compromise was reached. In early December, Tugerson's contract was sold to Dallas of the Texas League, and Tugerson dropped the lawsuit.

Schoolboy did pitch one game in a Bathers uniform. Three days before being optioned to Knoxville, Tugerson opened in an exhibition game against the Millington, Tennessee, Naval Air Station Hellcats at Jaycee Park in Hot Springs. Tugerson's scheduled start had been well publicized in the local Hot Springs paper and a parade had preceded the game. Tugerson pitched five complete innings, gave up five hits and two runs while striking out five and walking four. The final score was 17-5.

Following the well-publicized filing of the lawsuit, Schoolboy received a letter dated July 19th from Captain Herbert W. Wilson, Air Force Reserve, Berthold, North Dakota, who identified himself as Tugerson's squadron commander at Aloe Field, Victoria, Texas, where Tugerson pitched for the 347th Aviation Squadron team. Captain Wilson, having read of Schoolboy's plights in the local paper, strongly encouraged him to join the Minot Mallards in Minot, North Dakota, where he would have been welcome. Instead, Tugerson returned to Knoxville and finished the season.

Chapter 5

The Ever Changing Faces

The 1953 Smokies' roster was at times like a revolving door. Faces came and went. The goal was to improve the caliber of the players on the field, and as the season went along, that happened. The most difficult position to fill at the Class D level was pitcher. There weren't many gifts like Jim Tugerson being dropped in Pankovits' lap every day. Tugerson would leave twice during the season. The first time was in May when he was recalled to Hot Springs to pitch but was again denied the opportunity. The other time was in July when he left to file the law suit in Hot Springs. The rest of the time he was on the mound throwing hard strikes on his way to the best record in professional baseball that year. As the season progressed, Tugerson got more support at the plate and in the field, and especially in the bullpen. This chapter names the players who came and went and those who were there at the end.

To help put a team together Kitchens hired Vince Pankovits, age 33, who had played and managed in the Boston Braves organization in the minor leagues. Pankovits knew baseball people and baseball players and soon began to assemble a team. To be sure that they could field a team by the scheduled opening date of April 25th, Kitchens went so far as to place an ad in the April 8th issue of *The Sporting News* which read: "PLAYERS WANTED; Rookies, limited servicemen and veterans by Knoxville, Class D Mountain States League. Spring training now under way. Manager Vince Pankovits in charge." [Class D teams were limited to four veterans (over three years experience); six limited service players (one to three years experience); and the rest rookies.]

Vince Pankovits

Vince Pankovits, the first member of the 1953 Smokies, was there at the beginning and at the end and was an integral part of the team's success. He molded a team around Big Jim Tugerson. He saw Tugerson's first pitch to lead-off hitter George Giles of the Maryville-Alcoa Twins on opening day on April 25th at Hunt Field, and he saw Tugerson's last pitch in the play-off championship game against the Twins at Chapman Park the day after Labor Day.

Pankovits was a catcher, and he caught 90 games for the Smokies, but he also played outfield in 23 games. He played wherever there was a hole that needed filling and utilized his best players the same way. At the plate he led the team in doubles with 24 and batted in 78 runs while hitting .286. [Again for the unfamiliar, batting average is expressed in this way and defined as the ratio of hits to at bats; in other words batting average equals hits divided by the number of times at bat.]

Among the first players obtained by Pankovits was Joe Galen, who played some at third base for the Smokies Tri-State team in 1952. Galen played in 100 games for the Smokies and ended his season with a .253 batting average. Paul (Junior) Griffith, a third baseman/outfielder optioned from Greenville, Mississippi of the Cotton States League, and a 1952 Chicago Golden Gloves finalist, played 114 games with the Smokies. Griffith averaged .319, hit 18 doubles, knocked in 66 runs, and stole 35 bases. Jack Seagraves, who batted .352 in the Blue Ridge League in 1950, played in only two games.

Other early signers included Bill Forbes, a Cleveland, Ohio native, first baseman and power hitter bought from Hopkinsville of the Kitty League. Forbes played in 110 games and led the team in home runs (15) and RBIs (90) while averaging .294. Forbes, who finished second in the league among first basemen in fielding percentage, left the Smokies on August 15th. Bobby Grose, a second baseman bought from the Cincinnati Reds, was a steady playmaker for the Smokies, batting .282 while stealing 15 bases and knocking in 64 runs. Vic Steele, a second baseman, who was optioned from Greenville like Griffith, played in 31 games and hit .224.

Signing just a week before the opening game with the Maryville-Alcoa Twins was Charles Bradford, a free agent catcher who had been released by Columbia of the Sally League. Bradford played in 66 games and batted .301.

Catcher Porter Sheets, a power hitter optioned by the Cotton States' Hot Springs club, was returned to Hot Springs without playing. This was also the case with Raymond Sliga, an outfielder from Tifton, Georgia. Jose Lerma, a Mexican shortstop also optioned by Hot Springs, never played for the Smokies. Larry Maniuan, a Cuban outfielder from Sacramento of the Pacific Coast League, played in only three games and hit .333. Jack Campbell, an outfielder from Morristown with semi-pro experience, played in one game. At the same time this last group of players was signed, Pankovits and Kitchens sold outright Hugo Garcia, a Mexican outfielder obtained from Galveston, to the Norton Braves.

There were two other black players on the Smokies roster when the Tugersons arrived—David "Pepsi" Mobley, an outfielder who played in one game for Rock Hill in the Tri-State League in 1952, and Jimmy Brown, a second baseman. Mobley played in only 22 games for the Smokies and batted .269 while Brown played in 17 games before being traded to Morristown. These two black players were among the first African-Americans to don a Smokies uniform—ever. Jack Aragon, as the Smokies' general manager the previous year, had denounced the efforts of other teams in the Tri-State League that opposed black players in the league. The lone black player that played in the Tri-State League in 1952 was David Mobley.

Mobley left the 1953 Smokies in late May following the acquisition of Sonny Ashcraft who took playing time away from Mobley. He returned to Lancaster, South Carolina, and played semi-pro ball on an all-black team and never played organized ball again.

Besides the Tugersons, both right-handers, the only pitchers available to Pankovits on opening day were Bill Allen, Lloyd (Larry or Bud) Koehnke (pronounced Kinky), Pedro Iglesia, and Deryl Case. Allen, a right hander who had pitched for Rocky Mount in 1952, made only one appearance. Iglesia, a Cuban who came to the Smokies from Galveston of the Gulf Coast League, also made only one appearance. Koehnke pitched in 35 games, going 11-14 with an ERA of 5.47. He also had a win in the playoffs. Koehnke appeared at the plate in 52 games and hit a respectable .271. Ted Haynes, who played the outfield and first base and who also signed during late April, played in 18 games and batted .278.

Pitcher Paul Bubetz and shortstop Ronald McGamm arrived at Chapman Park in time for the first night game on May 8th, but neither ever played. Earl (Sonny) Ashcraft and Jerry Lindley, both outfielders, joined the club during May as did Jerome McGoldrick, a pitcher. Ashcraft played in 29 games and batted .347 before being traded to Hopkinsville of the Kitty League for Art Sabulsky. Lindley played 97 games for the Smokies and batted .314 with 21 doubles, 16 stolen bases, and 51 RBIs. McGoldrick made four appearances and ended with a record of 0-1. On June 17th Jack Jones, a third baseman who had just arrived from the Cincinnati Reds organization, would make his first start against Norton at Chapman Park, belting a double in four trips to the plate. Jones played in several games for the Smokies, but was traded to Harlan for Dick Carney; he ended the season with a cumulative average of .297.

Arriving at about the same time was Leonard (Bud) Scherman (also spelled Schuermann), a utility player who would be used to fill in for Grose at second base when Grose was at short. Scherman played in 53 games, 35 in the outfield and 18 in the infield while hitting a very respectable .330. Scherman went to Hopkinsville on July 21st when Ashcraft failed to report, but returned to Knoxville in mid-August when Forbes left. Pitcher Jim Williams, who was on the scene when pitching help started to arrive in late June, did not finish out the season and was released on August 2nd. He compiled a 5-2 record with an ERA of 5.95.

On Friday, June 19th, Ken Buckles and Robert

(Whitey) Diehl, right-handers with the Cincinnati Reds' Burlington (Iowa) club of the Class B Three-Eye League, arrived at Chapman Park in time to watch Koehnke eke out a win against Norton. Buckles pitched in 24 games, posted a record of nine wins and six losses and an ERA of 4.09. He also won a playoff game. He batted in 32 games, hit two home runs, batted in 8 runs, and finished the season at .194. Diehl made 18 appearances, had a 5-1 record, and an ERA of 5.34. At the plate, Diehl finished the season at .200.

Five days later, two more pitchers, both on option from the St. Louis Browns, arrived and joined the team at Big Stone Gap. Clarence Edward "Sweet Cakes" Isley, another black right-hander, who had defeated Don Newcombe in an exhibition game during the 1952 season, had gone 12-5 with the Cuban Giants of the Negro league. Isley, however, would make only seven appearances with the Smokies and end up 1-4. Fred Sarracino, a 17-year-old left-hander, who signed a pro contract after compiling a high school record of 29-1, would end the season with the Smokies at 3-2 and an ERA of 6.88.

Art Sabulsky, a 21-year-old, six feet three inch, 185-pound outfielder with the Philadelphia Athletics, arrived the same day as Isley and Sarracino. Sabulsky, whom Pankovits had seen play in the Kitty League at Hopkinsville the year before, was obtained in a trade that sent outfielder Sonny Ashcraft and pitcher Ray Glass to Hopkinsville. Sabulsky had set a record at Hopkinsville with 323 putouts and 23 assists while hitting .330. For the Smokies, Sabulsky played in 68 games and had 167 putouts and three assists, but he had 17 doubles and 56 RBIs while averaging .315. He was the only 1953 Smokies team member who also played for the 1954 Smokies at the new Knoxville Municipal Stadium.

Shortly after Independence Day, another pitcher arrived. James (Bud) Rengers made thirteen appearances, won three and lost one and finished with an ERA of 4.81. On July 16th, Richard (Dick) Carney was obtained from Harlan in a trade for Jack Jones to aid the Smokies' defense with his glove, but ended up making big contributions at the plate. He played 80 games for Harlan and 40 for the Smokies, hitting .221 with 14 doubles and 48 RBIs. On August 10th, David (Red) Clapp, came from the Inskip club in the Knoxville city league when a catcher was needed to replace the injured Bradford. Clapp played in thirteen games and hit .309 with 18 RBIs. Eight days later the last player to join the 1953 Smokies debuted. W. T. Wolfenbarger of Rutledge, Tennessee, who remained with the club only eight days, was added to play first base following the departure of Bill Forbes.

The line-up for the September 8th championship game had Len Scherman leading off and playing left field; the shortstop, Bobby Groce, hit second; playing 3rd and batting 3rd was Junior Griffith; batting clean-up and playing center field, Art Sabulsky; playing right field and batting 5th, Pankovits; playing second and batting 6th, Jerry Lindley; playing first base and hitting 7th, Charlie Bradford; catching and hitting 8th, Red Clapp; and pitching and batting last, Tugerson. The bullpen and bench players, who were not needed for that final game, included Buckles, Carney, Diehl, Koehnke, Rengers, and Sarracino. These were the guys that made it to the end.

Chapter 6

The Smokies Under Knox Baseball, Inc.

After the Knoxville City Council on January 30, 1953, voted 5-1 to begin razing the old Smithson Stadium to make way for the new Knoxville Municipal Stadium, a young entrepreneur with a family history in minor league baseball began laying plans to build a stadium the Smokies could use to play the 1953 season. Byron R. Kitchens knew where he could find the stadium. He just had to find some money, a franchise, and a baseball team.

Kitchens, as reported in *The Journal* and *The News-Sentinel* had $2,500 to invest, and he was able to find four other young risk-takers willing to match that amount. This would give him $12,500, enough to incorporate and purchase a franchise in the Class D Mountain States League run by Virgil Q. Wacks, a businessman and politician from Pennington Gap, Virginia. Kitchens knew that a franchise was available as the Hazard, Kentucky, club had been forced out due to poor attendance. Although *The Journal* and *The Sentinel* made frequent reference to the Kitchens' investors, neither paper ever identified them by name.

On March 14th of that year Kitchens made application for a Charter of Incorporation under the name Knox Baseball, Inc., the principal office of which was located at Chapman Highway, R.F.D., Seymour, Tennessee. The business to be transacted was "to operate a professional baseball club and generally to carry on the business of furnishing entertainment and incidental refreshment to the public." The stock issue was the standard 1,000 shares of common stock with no par value. The initial capital was $2,000. The application was signed by Kitchens, Knoxville attorney Robert S. Young, Jr., and Alberta H. Piper. It was drawn up by Knoxville attorney Lindsey Young, a notary public and brother of Robert. A copy of this certificate was filed March 23, 1953 at the Sevier County Register of Deeds.

In March, 1954, a year after Knox Baseball, Inc. was formed, William B. Reese, age 29, treasurer of the corporation, testified in an involuntary bankruptcy proceeding in Knoxville. He identified investors other than Kitchens and himself, as Joe Townsend, William Trainor, and a Captain Denham of the United States Air Force. Reese testified that each had an initial investment of $1,500; of this $7,500 investment, $1,650 was paid to the National Association for Baseball Leagues; $550 to the Mountain States League; $300 to Chapman Highway Park for first month's rent; and $1,450 to the Knoxville Utilities Board, $1,000 of which was a deposit for the estimated cost of $3,300 for wiring the light poles. Kitchens later dropped out and Captain Denham, who was transferred by the Air Force from Knoxville to Minnesota in October, 1953, took over as president.

In September, 1948, Clyde Huskey, age 33, President, Chapman Highway Park, Inc. purchased land on the east, or Sevier County, side of Chapman Highway near the intersection of Chapman Highway and Old Sevierville Pike. In December, 1958 this property was subdivided into seven commercial and 17 residential lots under the name Chapman Park Subdivision. There is no longer a visible trace of this ballpark.

This ballpark, which was believed to never have much more than bleacher seats and a wire backstop, apparently had been used for semi-pro county league games for some five years. Such leagues were popular in East Tennessee in the 1940's and 1950's. In Sevier County there were teams in Walden's Creek, Wears Valley, Knob Creek, Dumpling, and Dupont. Seymour obviously had a team as well. The best player that ever played for any of these teams was Ed Bailey who played for Dumpling and would later sign a contract with the Cincinnati Reds. Ironically, Bailey would be the starting catcher for the Reds when they met the Chattanooga Lookouts in an exhibition game to open the new Knoxville Municipal Stadium on April 7, 1954.

When I was 14 Sevierville tried unsuccessfully to get a team together, and I pitched one game for them. I also pitched a game for Walden's Creek when their regular starter was unavailable. These games were usually played on Saturday afternoons. Knoxville had a good city league. There were some good ball players spread around those leagues.

In an effort to legitimize my memory and to retain my sanity concerning Chapman Highway Park and the 1953 Smokies, I set out to find someone, anyone, who had similar recollections. I met an old outfielder who played for the Dupont team of the Sevier County league in the early 1950's. When I asked Edgar "Trubb" Gibson, a Seymour native, if he recalled the location of Chapman Highway Park where the Smokies played their games in 1953, he immediately responded, "Jim Tugerson," as if that name was synonymous with the specific answer I was seeking. I saw the same look in Trubb's eyes that I would see in the eyes of Tugerson's bullpen buddy, Ken Buckles, a week or so later. Trubb not only recalled the location of the ball park but related a story of having once stepped into the batter's box against Tugerson and almost getting a hit. The first baseman took away his line-drive hit by trapping the ball in the top of the mitt's webbing.

Kitchens made a deal with Clyde Huskey in which Knox Baseball, Inc. would renovate the ball park to a level suitable for minor league baseball and Huskey would be the General Manager, taking care of the day-to-day matters at the park. The park thereafter took on a new look. A covered grandstand with a ticket booth, office, locker rooms and showers were built. Dugouts were built and bleacher seats were added along the right field side. The base paths were cut, the infield seeded and a new fence was added. Poles with lights were erected, of course, to allow for the heavy schedule of night games.

A week before the opener, Kitchens issued an invitation to all baseball fans in the Knoxville and Sevierville areas to come out and see the ball park and observe the players during practice. He was eager for everyone to see the renovations and upgrades to the stadium and field, which were being overseen by Huskey. As it turned out Kitchens' invitation was a little premature. The Tugersons hit town a couple of days later, and this Smokies team was never the same.

The April 21st issue of *The News-Sentinel* ran the same wire photo of Jim and Leander in their Bathers uniforms which by now had become a stock item in the sports writers' world. The Smokies uniforms, like the Tugersons, arrived just in time. Two days before the opener, a photo of a smiling Vince Pankovits modeling his new uniform ran in *The News-Sentinel.*

Kitchens and his group had the new uniforms for the Smokies in time for the opener. Jack Aragon, the Knoxville Smokies General Manager the previous year, now the General Manager for the Maryville-Alcoa Twins, purchased the old Smokies' uniforms, stripped "Smokies" from the fronts, and had "Twins" sewn on in its place. In hindsight this alternative seemed entirely appropriate for what turned out to be a bizarre opening day.

The preparations were chaotic and last minute. Game time was not announced until Friday. The start time was changed from the evening to 3:00 p.m. as the lights and poles, although delivered, had not yet been installed at Hunt Field. The new manager for the Maryville-Alcoa Twins, Jim Poole, also did not show up until Friday.

Finally everything seemed to be in place for the season opener on Saturday, April 25, 1953, against the Twins at Hunt Field, including the probable starting lineups.

Pankovits announced the following Smokies lineup (in batting order): Lucas Lerma, short stop; Paul Griffith, center field; Bill Forbes, first base; Ted Haynes, right field; Vince Pankovits, catcher; Joe Galen, third base; David Mobley, left field; Bobby Groce, second base, and Jim Tugerson, pitcher.

Jim Tugerson got a wakeup call in the first inning of his first start with the Smokies, and Willie Kirkland, a young, strong black outfielder from Siluria, Alabama, rang the bell. An estimated opening day crowd of 1,000 fans watched Kirkland boom a high 400 foot 2-run homer over the right field fence in his first at bat in a professional baseball game. Kirkland, only nineteen and destined for nine years in the majors with the Giants and Indians, missed hitting the cycle by a double. [Once again for the unfamiliar, a cycle is hitting a single, double, triple, and home run in the same game.] He ended the game with three RBIs and was intentionally walked in the fifth. The Twins scattered nine more hits and won the game 9 to 5. Pankovits was tossed from the game in the 2nd after losing an argument on a double play in which he was caught off base. Pankovits left the game and put Bill Forbes in charge. Forbes immediately announced the game was being played under protest. The Smokies lost anyway, but the season was finally underway.

The confrontation between Kirkland and Tugerson initiated a competitive struggle that would last through the championship play-off game. There was always a slightly detectable smile on their faces when they faced one another. It was power against power, and it was special.

The second game of the season and the home opener for the Smokies at Chapman Highway Park against the Twins was set for Sunday at 2: 30 p.m. All six other teams in the Mountain States League were opening play on this Sunday. Morristown was at Kingsport; Norton was at Big Stone Gap; and Middlesboro was at Harlan.

The Smokies home opener included a little pre-game fanfare before more than 3,000 fans. The "Ole Coon

Hunter," Cas Walker, who had fought for baseball in Knoxville as a Knoxville City Councilman just four months before, was on hand to throw the first pitch. Walker, a Sevier County native, was neither a stranger to the Seymour crowd nor to the Mountain States League. The league president, Virgil Q. Wacks, was the person most influential in convincing Walker to build one of his supermarkets in Pennington Gap, Virginia, Wacks' hometown. Pennington Gap was also the hometown of Smokies manager, Vince Pankovits. Walker's catcher was Fred Atchley, a State Representative from Sevierville, and Sevierville Mayor Bob Ogle was the batter. *Growing up in Sevierville, Fred Atchley lived two doors from me, and Bob Ogle, a local attorney, was a member of my church. Both were big supporters of high school football.*

It would be a long afternoon for the Smokies—three hours and one minute long. Each member of the pitching staff except the Tugersons made an appearance. Bill Allen, Bud Koehnke, Pedro Iglesia, and Deryl Case—each shared in giving up 11 hits and 15 walks in the 14-12 loss to the Twins. Koehnke was charged with the "L". Kirkland was again the big gun for Maryville-Alcoa, belting two hits including a double and collecting two RBIs in the 9-run 2nd inning. Fortunately, the Smokies had Monday off but would be at Morristown for night games on Tuesday and Wednesday.

Big Jim and the Smokies got their first win on April 28th at Morristown 13-2. Leander followed his brother's lead with a win on the following night over Morristown 13-9, striking out six and walking five. With only one day's rest, Jim Tugerson won again at Alcoa, besting the Twins 7-4. Big Jim allowed six hits while striking out nine and walking five. In the second game of that two game series at Maryville-Alcoa, Leander, also pitching with only one day's rest, lost in relief of Bud Kochecke, 8-7. This was a wild and almost comical outing as the Smokies committed six errors, walked eight, and had two passed balls.

Both Jim and Leander were back on the mound for a Sunday afternoon double-header on May 3rd with the Middlesboro A's. Jim pitched a 4-hitter in the opener and bagged his 3rd "W," 3-2. Both of the A's runs were unearned. In the nightcap Leander helped his own cause and led all hitters with a homer and a double but needed help from his brother Jim to preserve the 16-12 win after pitching 8 2/3 innings. Leander ran out of steam in the top of the ninth inning when he gave up eight runs. He needed Big Jim to come in and get the last out for him, which he did. It was after these performances that *The Journal's* Tom Anderson suggested the nickname of Dark Stars for the team rather than the Smokies.

By the end of May, Big Jim was 8-2 and the Smokies, with a record of 19 wins and 14 losses, were in third place in the league standings, three games back of Maryville-Alcoa. Leander was 3-5 and would never pitch again. Like his brother, Leander seldom had more than two days rest between starts and had developed a sore arm, ultimately determined to be a torn muscle. He remained in Knoxville for another month, but would then go home to Florence Villa, Florida.

Things would get worse, however, before they got better. The Smokies were over $21,000 in debt and flat broke. Just how broke came to light on the evening of May 28th when the Smokies had to forfeit a game to Morristown when they ran out of baseballs in the 7th inning. There were appeals for those who had carted off any foul balls to return them, but these appeals fell on deaf ears. This story hit the AP and UPI wires and became a trivial story of national interest. Within five days Clyde Huskey had received about three dozen new baseballs from Montreal, Canada; Goldblude, Mississippi; Peoria, Illinois; LaCrosse, Wisconsin; Dearborn, Michigan; Norfolk, Virginia; Hot Springs, Arkansas; and Shreveport, Louisiana. All these appeared to have been sent by kids; however, one ball was received from a sporting goods store in Helena, Montana.

A group from Hazard, Kentucky, headed by Willie Dewahare, a Hazard department store executive, had offered to pay the Smokies $1,000 per game for one game each week or to buy the franchise outright. Of course this situation afforded several Knoxville sports writers the opportunity to vent their anger and frustration toward the "Chapman Park Seviers," as they liked to call them, and to yell over and over again, "We told you so!" In the view of a handful of these writers, this baseball club calling themselves the Knoxville Smokies was total blasphemy.

Tom Anderson in his column of May 31st in *The Journal* had ended his assault on the ball club with "...And so, as their boat limps away from Chapman Park's door, let us bid the Dark Stars bon voyage to Hazard, which, incidentally, is a rather frightening name for a team already in sore straits."

Chapter 7

The Smokies Under Grubb

Before Mr. Dewahare could write a check, Dr. Edgar Grubb, a prominent Knoxville eye, ear, nose, and throat specialist, along with a few unnamed investors, made a deal with the Mountain States League to take over the franchise. With the stroke of a pen, the Chapman Park Seviers had been magically transformed into that name they had been using all along—the Knoxville Smokies. The Smokies would continue to wear the same uniforms, would continue to play at Chapman Park, and even Clyde Huskey, who owned the park, could stay on if he liked, but now they had become the real Knoxville Smokies. Dr. Grubb identified the other investors as "friends of mine," but it was apparent that these were the same unnamed investors who had supported the notion of waiting to build a new stadium in Knoxville, voted on by the Knoxville City Council on January 30th.

When asked by *The News-Sentinel* about the possibility of higher class in the future, Dr. Grubb was quoted as saying, "I know the people of Knoxville, Knox County, and Sevier County where the park is located are not too happy with Class D baseball. But I'm afraid the people will just have to accept that class ball for the present until we can get higher class ball. I'm told the class isn't much under that played in the Tri-State League which was in Knoxville from 1946 through 1952. In fact, Jack Aragon told me that both his team and Knoxville's team are about the equal of any team Knoxville fielded in the Tri-State League."

Dr. Grubb knew that Big Jim Tugerson was the heart and soul of the Knoxville Smokies, and he was the reason people came to see the Smokies. With this in mind he laid plans to honor Tugerson with "Big Jim Tugerson Night" on Friday, June 5th. The opponent would be the league leading

Maryville-Alcoa Twins. The same day the plans were announced to fete Jim, Leander was told by a physician he was through for the season due to soreness in his pitching arm that would not go away.

Some 500 black fans came from Knoxville to Seymour by the busloads and were admitted free to honor Tugerson. In addition, there were 732 paid fans in attendance. Gifts for Tugerson had started arriving at Chapman Park the day before, and many brought gifts on game night. The gifts that night, presented to Tugerson after the game, included a radio, fishing equipment, clothing, and 16 wrapped gifts. The gifts were a way of showing admiration for his talents and gratitude for his having recently returned to Knoxville from Hot Springs.

Tugerson, of course, was at his best. Big Jim allowed a bloop single in the first and then pitched no-hit ball the rest of the way. He struck out fifteen, walked four, and ended up with his tenth win against three losses. The final score was 4-2. Even Willie Kirkland went 0 for 4.

A couple of days after Tugerson's dramatic win, league president Virgil Q. Wacks announced that Dr. Grubb, as the result of a vote by the league's directors, was designated the sole owner of baseball territorial rights in the Knoxville area. Previously it was believed the rights were shared equally by Knoxville and the Maryville-Alcoa club. George M. Trautman, president of the National Association of Professional Baseball Leagues (minors), settled the issue by explaining that a franchise gave protection rights within a 10-mile radius (of Knoxville) and that Hunt Field in Alcoa was located 13½ miles from Knoxville. This vote not only gave Dr. Grubb and his investors territorial rights for 1953 but for 1954 as well. These owners would be allowed to field a team at the new Knoxville Municipal Stadium the following year, and this team would be of the highest class ball Dr. Grubb could land.

On June 14th, *The News-Sentinel* published league statistics for pitching and hitting for the games through June 7th, which was just past the quarter mark of the season.

[Compilation of statistics always lagged behind a week or so, and they just couldn't keep pace with Tugerson. At the time these numbers were released, he had actually recorded 12 wins.] At this point, Tugerson led the league in complete games with 10; the most wins with 8; the most innings with 90; and the most strikeouts with 97. Leander, who was inactive by the end of May, led the league in most base hits allowed with 103. Bud Koehnke was leading the league in walks with 61. Ned Jilton of Kingsport had 7 wins without a loss. Walt Dixon, an outfielder and playing manager of the Norton Braves was leading the circuit in hitting with a .447 average; Nap Reys, playing manager of the Morristown club, was second at .444; Sonny Ashcraft and Big Stone Gap's Frank Hensley were tied for third at .405. The Braves also led in team hitting at .308 and Dixon also led in total hits with 68, total bases with 120, and was tied for most home runs with 12.

During the first three weeks of June, Tugerson seldom pitched with more than two days rest, and more often than not, only one day. Behind Tugerson was Koehnke, who was unpredictable and frequently wild, but who would win almost half his starts. Beyond Koehnke there was not much help. The rest of the bullpen consisted of Jim Williams, Jerome McGoldrick, and Pedro Iglesia.

Without a doubt, Pankovits, Tugerson, and Koehnke were glad to welcome pitchers Ken Buckles, Whitey Diehl, Edward Isley, and Freddie Sarracino during the fourth week of June. Help had finally arrived. Help at the plate and in the field had also shown up in the cleats of Art Sabulsky.

Buckles got his first start on a hot, Sunday afternoon at Kingsport, where Tugerson had lost the night before with a good effort 8-4. Tugerson had fanned ten, walked only two, and scattered ten hits. The Smokies offense had provided some bat support with thirteen hits but had stranded as many runners. Tugerson had been beaten by the Cherokees' Ned Jilton, pushing his record to 10-1. Tugerson's record slipped to 13-5.

Jesus Gonzales, the Cherokees second baseman, lined Buckles first pitch, a fastball down and in, down the left field line like a cannon shot for a double, one of seventeen he would hit that year. Buckles had gotten a wakeup call similar to that received by Tugerson back on April 25th except it was Jesus Gonzales, not Willie Kirkland. To make matters worse, he was introduced to Leo "Muscle" Shoals, Kingsport's manager and first baseman. Muscle, 33 years old at that time, started playing minor league baseball when Buckles was a 4-year-old back in Iowa. He would end his career in 1955 with 362 home runs and would be called "the Babe Ruth of minor league baseball." In 1953 Shoals hit 27 doubles, 7 triples, and 30 homers while batting .427 to lead the league. Muscle presented an intimidating figure with his barrel-chested build and big arms with cut-off sleeves. Walter Dixon, the manager and first baseman of the Norton Braves, had better numbers than Shoals except for his average which was 12 points under Shoals.

Buckles pitched well, protecting a 5-3 lead until the 9th when, with two on, Pankovits relieved him with Tugerson. Buckles complained, but it was pointless. Pankovits was going with his ace. Unbelievably, Ned Jilton pinch-hit a 3-run homer, one of two he hit all year, over the hedgerow in right field for a 6-5 win. No one could believe it, especially not Tugerson. He had been beaten by Jilton twice in less than 24 hours, and what was worse, he had three losses in a row. His record was now 13-6.

After the game, Buckles glared at Tugerson and threw a shoe against a locker to register his frustration and anger at Tugerson for costing him the win. According to Buckles, Tugerson, as he walked by whistling on his way to the shower, told him he was sorry, but to shake it off, that he would win more for him than he would lose. Buckles had no response. Again, Tugerson's words were prophetic. Before the season was over Big Jim would win three games for Buckles, two with his arm and one with the bat, but he did not allow any more losses.

After the losses at Kingsport, the team headed for Big Stone Gap where they split a double-header, losing the opener 4-0 and winning the late game 8-4. Before returning home to Chapman Park, Clarence Edward "Sweet Cakes" Isley would get his first start at Norton, losing 12-5. Sarracino would pitch two scoreless one-hit innings at Norton, the first since joining the Smokies.

Back at home with four days rest, Tugerson pitched a 2-hit shutout against Middlesboro, striking out thirteen, and winning 7-0. His win total now was at fourteen against seven losses. After dropping the second game of the Middlesboro series and the first of a 2-games series with the Twins, the Smokies won three straight—one at Maryville-Alcoa and two over Big Stone Gap. Buckles got his first win at Big Stone Gap 10-5, giving up 10 hits but aided his cause with two singles. The following night Fred Sarracino, the 17-year-old who had signed a $3,000 contract with the Baltimore Orioles, pitched the Smokies to a 9-2 win over Big Stone Gap at Chapman Park in his first pro start.

Buckles got his second win the last day of June at Middlesboro in relief of Jim Williams who had relieved Whitey Diehl, the starter, early on. Buckles, who pitched 4 2/3 innings, secured his win with a game-tying 2-run homer in the eighth inning. The Smokies scored three unearned runs in the ninth to win 12-9.

On the same day as Buckles' win at Middlesboro, another kind of action was initiated that would result in future and unprecedented humiliation for this team trying so hard to win. A petition was filed that day in United States District Court by eight creditors of Knox Baseball, Inc., the former owner of the Smokies. Dr. Grubb was not named in the petition as he did not absorb any of the debt when he bought the franchise. This petition was expected to force the previous organization into involuntary bankruptcy. A search of the U. S. District Bankruptcy Court records confirmed that an involuntary bankruptcy petition was filed against Knox

Baseball, Inc. on June 30, 1953. The petition contained only the names of the eight creditors and identified no corporate officers other than Byron Kitchens. Later testimony, however, identified all the investors.

At the end of May, the Smokies had been in third place only three games back of Maryville-Alcoa. At the end of June, the Smokies were still in third place but now found themselves nine games behind Maryville-Alcoa. Kingsport, 2 ½ games out in May, were now 1 ½ games out. Second place was a much better place to be in the Mountain States League when it came playoff time as the first place team played the third place team while the second place team played the fourth place team. This was especially true since Maryville-Alcoa had been in first place since opening day and was considered the strongest team in the league. The months of July and August presented an almost overwhelming challenge for all but Tugerson. He just kept pitching and winning.

1953 Knoxville Smokies

Front: Rengers, Sarracino, Pankovits, Jones, Griffith

Rear: Lindley, Sabulsky, Diehl, Grose, Galen, Tugerson, Forbes, Williams, Koehnke

Chapter 8

The July-August Run

Tugerson got his 15th win in the second game of the series at Middlesboro, 6-4, with ten strikeouts and two walks on July 1st. The Smokies dropped the next outing 14-11 at Morristown behind starter "Sweet Cakes" Isley, relieved early by Williams, then Buckles, then Diehl. Isley, who allowed a whopping eight runs in the first, was the losing pitcher. Tugerson, who sometimes played first or the outfield, or more frequently pinch hit when not pitching, hit one of his five home runs for the year. Tugerson, a good hitter, had 182 at bats and hit .308 with 35 RBIs during the season. In the second game at Morristown, Tugerson was back on the mound in relief of Buckles who pitched 8 1/3 innings. The winning run came in the 13th off the bat of Jack Jones who hit a solo home run. [Buckles, even though he did not get the win, neither did he get the loss, and was reminded of Tugerson's words, "I'll win more for you than I'll lose."] The Red Sox manager, Nap Reyes, played the game under protest after he noticed that the Smokies manager-catcher, Vince Pankovits, who had been tossed in the 5th, was sitting in the stands. The win (10-9) stood, however, for the Smokies, and for Tugerson, his sixteenth.

The last series of the first half was a two-game tilt with the Twins on a home and home basis. The first game was at Hunt Field where the Smokies dropped a slugfest, 16-12. In the second game that evening at Chapman Park, the last of the first half, "Sweet Cakes" Isley again was bombarded in the first for five runs. Obviously, Isley was the eventual loser as the Smokies lost, 8-5. These two losses dropped Knoxville to fourth place in the league standings, 11 ½ games back of Maryville-Alcoa.

The league All-Star game between all-stars from the

other seven teams against the first-place Maryville-Alcoa Twins at Hunt Field was scheduled for Thursday, July 9th, even though the second half of the season kicked off four days earlier. Knoxville opened the second half with four games against Morristown, two at home, then four at the Red Sox diamond. Tugerson, as he had in the first half, started the first game and won his seventeenth against seven losses with a 3-hitter, 5-1. Tugerson also led all hitters with a 2-run homer and a single in four trips to the plate, knocking in three of the five runs. This win put the Smokies in a tie with the Norton Braves for third.

The following night, again at Chapman Park, Buckles pitched his first complete game and got the win in the bottom half of the ninth when the Smokies rallied to score four in a come-from-behind victory, 7-6. In pre-game ceremonies, Mary Lee Thomas of Sevierville, a University of Tennessee majorette, was selected Queen of Knoxville Baseball from among six candidates for the title.

Mary Lee Thomas was one of four UT majorettes from Sevierville at that time. In the summer of 1953, I watched them practice in front of the Shanton house on Bruce Street in Sevierville. I had a huge crush on one of them, Betty Kay Shanton, but then she was 9 or 10 years my senior. I would learn 55 years later that Carl Widseth, Buckles' teammate at Davenport High School (Iowa), and a legendary basketball player at the University of Tennessee, married one of those majorettes. I would share that information with Buckles, who never met Widseth's wife. Interestingly, it was Widseth's death in Minneapolis on December 26, 2007, that enabled me to find Buckles through the Internet. It now seems fitting that Buckles was the winning pitcher the night Mary Lee Thomas was crowned.

The third game against the Red Sox, played at Morristown, pitted Freddie Sarracino, the young pitcher fresh out of a Pennsylvania high school, against the 6th place club. Sarracino pitched 8 1/3 innings before being relieved by Jim Williams. Jack Jones, the Smokies third baseman again swung a big stick, knocking in four runs with two homers and two singles in four trips to the plate. This win nudged Knoxville into third place. Knoxville's fourth straight win over the Red Sox earned Tugerson his 18th "W," but he had to feel indebted to Art Sabulsky who drove in five runs with two home runs and two singles. Len Scherman and Pankovits also had a homer and a single each. The final score was 13-9. This win helped solidify the Smokies hold on third place for the All-Star break.

Muscle Shoals of Kingsport had been selected to manage the All-Stars against Manager Jim Poole's Maryville-Alcoa Twins at Hunt Field in Alcoa. Six of the 21 players selected for the All-Star team were unanimous choices by all seven managers (Maryville-Alcoa manager Bill Poole was excluded from the voting.). Of course, Tugerson was one of the six. The only other Knoxville player selected by vote was slugging first baseman Bill Forbes. Pankovits was selected as an alternate catcher after he had refused to vote for himself in order to make the team.

The Mountain States League All-Stars defeated Maryville-Alcoa, 10-7, in eleven innings. Tugerson pitched three innings in relief but got no decision. He played the role of a slugger in this All-Star tilt rather than chalking up a win or save as a pitcher by hitting a 3-run homer. Others who homered in this game were the league's three leaders—Walt Dixon of Norton, Muscle Shoals of Kingsport, and Willie Kirkland of Maryville-Alcoa. Prior to the contest, Mary Lee Thomas, who just three weeks before had been crowned Queen of Knoxville Baseball, added the title of Queen of the Mountain States League to her accolades. She was selected by a four-judge panel from among six candidates.

Knoxville was at Harlan the night following the All-Star game against "the other Smokies," where they continued their winning ways. "Sugar Cakes" Isley would get his only win in a Smokies uniform. Although Isley walked ten in 4

2/3 innings, Williams came on in relief, finished the game, and recorded a save. Harlan stranded fifteen runners. Knoxville stranded ten but got good RBI production from Sabulsky, Pankovits, Lindley, and Jones to record the win, 12-5, their fifth straight to begin the second half. The Smokies extended the win streak to six the following night at Harlan with a 16-3 win.

With this win streak signs of hope, optimism, and even enthusiasm started to surface, some from unexpected sources. The Sunday, July 12th issue of The News-Sentinel promoted a double-header being played that day against the second-place Kingsport Indians and Tugerson's quest for win number nineteen. Dr. Grubb was quoted as saying the club was "well set now" to make a run in the second half of the season. Dr. Grubb was further quoted as saying, "Incidentally, I think a lot of Knoxville fans might be pleasantly surprised with the brand of ball we play in this league. For 50 cents (bleacher seat) they can get a lot of baseball today."

On Sunday, July 12th the second-place Kingsport Cherokees rolled into Chapman Highway Park for the first of two double-headers played on consecutive days. Tugerson won the first, a seven inning affair, 3-2, allowing only three hits including a homer in the 7th by Muscle Shoals, the slugging icon of the minors. Tugerson improved his record with this win, in which he gave up no walks and only three batters reached first, to 19 wins and seven losses. In the nightcap, Buckles pitched well for 6 1/3 innings when Tugerson came on in relief and got the save. [Buckles again heard those words forever etched in his memory, "I'll win more for you than I'll lose."]

The space afforded the coverage of this double-header which moved the Knoxville Smokies to one game behind the second-place Kingsport club by The News-Sentinel was the most given the team the entire season. It was a single column, but it ran from top to bottom, ending with a full-length photograph of Tugerson in his wind-up. The win was the eighth straight and the twelfth out of the Smokies' last fourteen games. Harold Harris' account of these occurrences was the most upbeat rendition offered by the Knoxville press all year.

The Smokies swept the second double-header from the Cherokees the next day as well, allowing them to take sole possession of the second-place slot that had been occupied by Kingsport for so long. In the opener, Koehnke pitched only two innings before leaving with a sore shoulder. Sarracino came on in relief, pitched five innings, and closed a 7-hit 4-0 shutout. In the last game, Tugerson relieved the middle reliever, Buckles, in the seventh with bases loaded and nobody out in a 2-2 game. Tugerson got out of the jam with no runs scoring, but the Tribe picked up a run in the eighth and took the lead 3-2. Sabulsky doubled in the ninth with bases loaded and the game was over with the final score, 4-3. The win was Tugerson's 20th against seven losses. After winning ten straight, the Smokies were now six games behind the league-leading Twins.

Tugerson left Chapman Park after hurling his 20th win and traveled to Hot Springs in connection with his lawsuit. He returned in four days and pitched the fifth day at Kingsport, where he had a dismal outing, going only 3 2/3 innings before being relieved by Koehnke, who lost the game, 11-10, in the bottom of the ninth. In Tugerson's absence, the Smokies had extended the win streak to eleven at Norton, 6-5, before losing to Norton the next night, 6-2.

Following the Norton series, the Smokies would win two more games against Harlan at Chapman before Tugerson's sub-par performance at Kingsport. Bud Koehnke pitched a 6-hit 3-1 win in the opening game of the double-header against Harlan on July 17th. An estimated crowd of 600 watched the Smokies trounce Harlan 19-8 with fifteen hits in the second game. These wins put Knoxville 5 ½ games back of Maryville-Alcoa and a game ahead of third-place Kingsport. These wins also gave the Smokies a record 13 wins out of the last 14 games to go with the record 11-game win streak.

Tugerson, back in pre-lawsuit form, extracted some vengeance from the Norton Braves for ending the Smokies winning streak in his absence by hurling a 3-hit 7-0 shutout at Chapman Highway Park on July 20th. His supporting cast pelted 15 hits. Joe Galen and Dick Carney, who had reported from Harlan in a trade that sent Jack Jones to Harlan, each had three hits. Tugerson was now twenty-one and seven, but the Smokies had slipped back into third behind Kingsport. Following this win, "Sugar Cakes" Isley (1-4) was returned to the St. Louis Browns who sent him on to Danville, Illinois.

Isley's departure left Big Jim as the only black player on the Smokies' roster. Leander hadn't pitched since May and after being unable to rehabilitate his sore arm went home to Florence Villa in early July. David "Pepsi" Mobley, who had opened the season in right field, had left the team in late May, and Jimmy Brown, an infielder, was traded to Morristown at about the same time Mobley went home.

Ironically, Mobley broke the color barrier twice in successive years in two different leagues. On August 26, 1952 Mobley, a native of Lancaster, South Carolina got two at bats with the Rock Hill Chiefs against the Knoxville Smokies at Rock Hill. Both these clubs had been members of the Tri-State League the previous year. Mobley went 1-for-2 that night at Rock Hill but never got to appear in another game. The Tri-State League experienced the same kind of opposition from one or more of its teams that the Cotton States League experienced in 1953. With those two plate appearances Mobley became the first black player to play in a Tri-State League game. In 1953 he became one of the first black players to appear in the Mountain States League.

On July 22nd, between Tugerson's shut outs against Norton and Big Stone Gap, a story appeared in The News-

Sentinel that the Hot Springs Bathers, who still held Tugerson's contract, revealed the club was negotiating with two major league clubs for his sale, and "...believe he's ready for major league competition." H. M. Britt, president of the Bathers, said he was trying to sell Tugerson outright, but refused to identify the interested major league clubs. He later acknowledged that a Pittsburgh Pirate scout had looked at Tugerson. Billy Meyer, Pirates scout and former manager, later confirmed that he had scouted Tugerson. He was quoted as saying Tugerson was difficult to scout because he could "coast" against most of the hitting he faced in the Cotton States League. Meyer had never observed Tugerson in a situation where he had really had to bear down. The other club scouting Tugerson was never named by Britt, however; Joe Sewell, a scout for the Cleveland Indians, was at the August 2nd game against Morristown which Tugerson lost.

After a couple of rain-outs, and with two days rest, Tugerson pitched his second consecutive 3-hit shut out, this time against Big Stone Gap, 5-0. This win upped his season record to twenty-two wins. Buckles suffered his second loss in the second game of this double-header, 8-5, in eleven innings. The Smokies extended this losing streak to four with three road losses at Middlesboro. Koehnke lost the first 6-4; Williams lost a laugher 22-1; and Buckles got his third loss with a 7-3 score.

As expected, Tugerson stopped the skid July 27th with a home win against Middlesboro, 11-4, recording his 23rd win. All four runs scored off Tugerson in this game came in the sixth inning, stopping his scoreless inning streak at home at twenty-one. Rengers followed Tugerson's win in the nightcap with a 10-5 loss, in which Sarracino, Diehl, Williams, and Buckles all pitched in relief. In the third game of this home stand, Dick Carney, acquired through a trade for his glove, proved to be an unlikely hero at the plate in the Smokies 6-3 win. Carney, who had knocked in a run in the sixth with a single, came to bat in the eighth with the score tied at 3-3. He doubled in the winning runs and then scored himself off Joe Galen's double.

The Smokies then took two games from the Big Stone Gap Rebels 12-7 and 13-7. Whitey Diehl picked up a win in the second game, pitching five complete innings. His college basketball teammate, Buckles, relieved Diehl in the sixth and got credit for the save. On the last day of July, Tugerson suffered his eighth loss of the season against the first-place Maryville-Alcoa Twins, 8-5, at Chapman Highway Park. Tugerson's nemesis, Willie Kirkland, went 3-for-5 including a triple and knocked in two runs. Tugerson batted in two runs in the bottom of the eighth to tie the game at 5-5, but the Twins sealed the win with three runs in the ninth. This loss put Tugerson's record at 23-8, made the Smokies at 56-43, and landed the team in third place 9 ½ games back of the Twins. This loss was his only loss in July after nine wins. Only one umpire showed up for this game. Smokies pitchers Koehnke and Buckles and Twins pitcher Charlie Lovell were recruited to assist the single umpire.

In the second game of the Twins series, played at Hunt Field, Koehnke pitched eight complete innings before being relieved in the ninth by Rengers, Sarracino, and Buckles. The Smokies scored six runs in the eighth to take a 10-9 lead, led by Pankovits with a bases-loaded double. With the bases loaded in the ninth, Sarracino struck out Kirkland, and Buckles threw one pitch that ended in a double play to win the game.

Tugerson suffered his second consecutive loss against Morristown on August 2nd. The game was played at Leslie Street Park in east Knoxville "so the people who don't have transportation to Chapman Highway Park can see the winningest pitcher in baseball," Dr. Grubb had been quoted as saying. Advance tickets had been put on sale at the east Knoxville recreation center and American Legion. Attendance was estimated at 650, well below what was anticipated. Tugerson pitched only four innings and gave up four runs as did Sarracino and Rengers, producing a final score of 12-3. The worst part was that Tugerson lost with Cleveland Indians scout Joe Sewell observing from the stands. This loss put Tugerson's record at 23 wins and 9 losses.

The day after Tugerson's loss against Morristown, pitcher Jim Williams was released outright as "an economy move." Williams (5-2) finished his season with the 1953 Knoxville Smokies with an ERA of 5.95.

After the Leslie Park faux pas against the Red Sox, Buckles started the next game back at Chapman Highway Park. Buckles pitched a complete game, scattering twelve hits among four strikeouts and three walks, ending it at 8-5. He benefited from Sabulsky's three RBIs and the team's five stolen bases. Buckles' record went to 5-2 with this win.

The Smokies traveled next to Middlesboro where they had lost three straight just over a week before, and this trip was no different, dropping both games, 8-2 and 3-2. Koehnke lost the first, pitching five innings before being relieved by Diehl. The Athletics scored four runs in the fifth and maintained the lead until the game was called in the 8th because of rain. Tugerson was tagged with his 10th loss in the second game, his third straight, losing it in the 11th inning. The Smokies seemed to be jinxed at Middlesboro. They could not win there, and fortunately, this was the last time they would play there. The return home against Kingsport did not exactly spark another winning streak as Buckles gave up nine hits and five runs in the first four innings, including a 2-run homer by Muscle Shoals. Diehl and Sarracino relinquished eight more hits and five more runs before the dust settled. The final score was 10-4.

The next day, August 7th, the annual North-South All-Star game was played at J. Fred Johnson Park in Kingsport. The North was made up of the Virginia and Kentucky teams—Big Stone Gap, Norton, Harlan, and Middlesboro while the South consisted of players from Kingsport, Knoxville, Maryville-Alcoa, and Morristown.

Tugerson was the only Knoxville player selected for the game which the South lost 9-8 in the eleventh.

At this juncture, Knoxville was still in third place, four games behind Kingsport and eleven games back of Maryville-Alcoa. Knoxville was at Big Stone Gap the day following the All-Star tilt where they lost the first game 18-12. Tugerson got another shut-out in the second game (8-0) notching his 24th victory against nine losses. On that same night a few miles up the road at Norton, Willie Kirkland of the Twins tied two Mountain States League records when he hit three home runs and knocked in ten runs. The homers gave Kirkland thirty for the season, two behind the leader, Norton's Walt Dixon.

Jim Rengers picked up a win upon the Smokies return to Chapman Highway Park against Middlesboro, 13-5, on Monday, August 10th. Rengers allowed eight hits, fanned twelve, and walked four. He got huge support at the plate from his power-slugging first baseman, Bill Forbes, and his shortstop, little Dick Carney. Forbes went 3-for-5 with a homer and five RBIs while Carney went 4-for-4 with a homer and four RBIs. David "Red" Clapp, a catcher, joined the Smokies this game after Charlie Bradford went out with an injury. Clapp had played for Inskip in the Knoxville City League. Bud Koehnke was charged with the loss in the second game, allowing all seven runs scored by the Athletics—three in the first and four in the fifth. Buckles and Tugerson pitched in relief in a losing cause with a final score of 7-6. Knoxville had twelve hits but stranded ten.

The Kingsport Cherokees handed Tugerson his 11th and final defeat, 6-5, a 13- inning affair at Kingsport on August 12th. Tugerson gave up 20 hits during this marathon, and Kingsport left 20 runners on base. After this exhausting effort, Tugerson's record was now twenty-four wins and eleven losses. Whitey Diehl started the next day against Kingsport and pitched eight solid innings before being lifted for a pinch hitter in the ninth inning. Manager Vince

Pankovits doubled across the tying and winning runs in the final frame. Diehl, who gave up seven hits, struck out ten, and walked nine, was credited with the win but was given some excellent relief work from—you guessed it—Tugerson. Tugerson retired the side in order the bottom of the ninth. [Undoubtedly, Tugerson's declaration to Buckles eight weeks earlier, also at Kingsport, was ringing in Whitey's ears.]

Back at home the following night, the next game against the Big Stone Gap Rebels was one that all the 1953 Knoxville Smokies, especially Ken Buckles, would want to forget. After five innings, the Smokies led 18-4, having scored two runs in the first and third, eight in the fourth, and six more in the fifth. Then, in an apparent effort to rest the regulars, Pankovits substituted a new team, putting some players in positions they did not normally play. Big Stone Gap scored fourteen runs, including six in the eighth and five in the ninth to put the game into extra innings. Big Stone Gap's Herman Thompson homered in the seventh, tripled in the ninth to score the tying run, and doubled in the tenth to drive across the winning run. Knoxville was held to one hit during the last five frames. Buckles, who was catching until the tenth, pitched to Thompson who knocked in what turned out to be the winning run, and Buckles was charged with the loss. This 37-run game was the highest scoring of the season.

Some semblance of reality was restored the following evening (although not entirely) as this game, also against Big Stone Gap, produced 25 runs. It also produced Tugerson's 25th win.

It was August 16th and there were fifteen games left to play. Bill Forbes, the team's most prolific slugger, had left the team without explanation. Forbes' departure marked the return of Len Scherman from Hopkinsville. With their 59-51 record, the Smokies were in third place—two games behind Kingsport, and ten games back of Maryville-Alcoa. The team had been locked into third place for so long it seemed unlikely that it would overcome Kingsport's grip on the slot. All was not bleak however. Tugerson was 25 and 11 and "Mary Lee Thomas Night" had been scheduled for August 19th at Chapman Highway Park when the Smokies would again play the league-leading team from Blount County.

On Sunday, August 16th, the Smokies lost their 52nd game to the Morristown Red Sox at Morristown. Knoxville rebounded the next day and beat Morristown 4-1 with Buckles pitching his best game. Buckles gave up the one run in the sixth and allowed only four hits. The game went into extra frames, and Buckles pitched all resulting 12 innings without relief. Tugerson played first base the last three innings and belted a 3-run homer, called the best play in baseball by future Smokies and Baltimore Orioles manager Earl Weaver, to seal the win. [Buckles surely heard Tugerson's prophetic words once again.] With Buckles' pitching, Tugerson's hitting, and Kingsport's losing to Maryville-Alcoa, 22-6, Knoxville and Kingsport were tied for second place.

The Maryville-Alcoa Twins were back at Chapman Highway Park the following evening and came from behind to win big, 14-8. Jim Rengers, the starter, gave up seven hits and eight runs in 3 2/3 innings while his relief, Fred Sarracino, allowed six hits and six runs in the remaining 5 1/3 innings. Sarracino got the loss. W. T. Wolfenbarger, a recent addition to the Smokies roster from Rutledge, Tennessee, played first base and went 0-for-4 at the plate.

The following night was the last scheduled regular season game Maryville-Alcoa played at Chapman Highway Park. It was "Mary Lee Thomas Night" in honor of her winning not only the Queen of Knoxville Baseball crown, but also the title of Mountain States League Queen, awarded at the All-Star game in Alcoa on July 9th. Miss Thomas was scheduled to represent the league at the Minor League Convention in Atlanta the following winter.

Mary Lee Thomas
1953 Knoxville Smokies Queen

Tugerson started a little wild, walking four and giving up three hits in the first two innings. After the second, he settled down and pitched one-hit ball, winning easily and big, 16-2. This was Tugerson's 26th win against 11 losses, but Knoxville was still in third place. [Before this game began, the same troupe of University of Tennessee majorettes from Sevierville that I watched practice performed in front of the grandstand.]

Knoxville was at Norton the next two nights, losing the first game 7-4 with Koehnke taking the loss, but winning the second, 11-1. Knoxville and Kingsport were again tied for second.

While the Smokies were on the road at Norton, the Kansas City Monarchs and the Birmingham Black Barons of the Negro American League slipped into town and played at Chapman Highway Park on Friday, August 21st. Black fans were bused from Knoxville to the Seymour ball park the same way that they had been bused all year to see the Smokies play. Some 1200 fans, the largest crowd at the park since "Jim Tugerson Night," saw the Monarchs nip the Barons 8-7. An added attraction at the game was the Flying Nesbits, the only black acrobatic-comedian troupe, who entertained the fans before the game and between innings. An intriguing irony in the seating arrangements was put in place for this game; a section of the grandstand and the right field bleachers were reserved for white fans attending the game.

On Saturday night, August 22nd, Tugerson tied the league record for wins with twenty-seven. The record was held by Johnny Podres who, at the age of 19, had set the record at Hazard in 1951. Podres also had 228 strikeouts and an ERA of 1.67 that year at Hazard. In 1955, Podres won two games, including the seventh, in the only World Series the Brooklyn Dodgers ever won over the New York Yankees. Tugerson tied Podres' Mountain States League record against Harlan at Chapman Highway Park with a final score of 20-3. There was another "man of the hour" player in this game besides Tugerson. Red Clapp, the Knoxville catcher filling in for the injured Charlie Bradford, homered, tripled, and doubled twice to drive in eight runs. Knoxville remained tied with Kingsport for second.

The next win against Harlan the following day should have been dubbed "Whitey Diehl Day" as Diehl, after relieving Jim Rengers in the sixth, held Harlan scoreless and allowed only one hit. Diehl also homered and singled, driving in three runs, to lead the Smokies at the plate. Knoxville and Kingsport remained deadlocked.

Two days after tying Podres' league record for wins, Tugerson broke the record by virtue of his win at Harlan 8-7. Tugerson had plenty of support with Sabulsky's 2-run homer and triple as well as Scherman's homer and Pankovits' bases-loaded double that scored four runs in the eighth. This win put Knoxville in second, a game ahead of Kingsport. Knoxville dropped the second game at Harlan (9-3) and the Smokies and Cherokees were tied again.

Knoxville then swept a 3-game series from the Norton Braves at Norton. Buckles won the first game of a double-header (6-5) allowing eleven hits, but getting good run support from Sabulsky, Clapp, and Wolfenbarger. Buckles roommate and best friend, Whitey Diehl, won the nightcap 2-1, pitching a 6-hitter. The run production again came from Sabulsky and Clapp. After the double-header wins, the Smokies were a game up on Kingsport.

Tugerson got his 29th win and 7th shutout by pitching a 2-hitter in game three at Norton, winning three runs to none. All the scoring in the game occurred in the 8th when Knoxville scored three unearned runs after Norton manager Walt Dixon booted Grose's grounder giving Sabulsky and Clapp the opportunity to knock in runs. With this win, the Smokies were two games ahead of Kingsport; and with two games left, they had clinched at least a tie.

The Smokies lost their last two games at Morristown 13-4 and 8-6. Those losses did not affect the standings as Kingsport split its last two games. Knoxville ended up with

70 wins and 55 losses while Kingsport closed out the regular season at 69-56. The first-place Maryville-Alcoa Twins finished with 78 wins and 47 losses.

After 125 games, Norton and Morristown were deadlocked at 63 wins and 62 losses each. These teams played each other at Morristown in an extra game the day after the regular season to determine which team would play Knoxville in the playoffs set to begin on August 31st. Morristown made the playoffs by virtue of an 8-2 win over Norton. Maryville-Alcoa would meet Kingsport at Hunt Field in Alcoa, and Knoxville was slated to play at Morristown.

Big Jim Tugerson had pitched 330 innings, recorded 286 strikeouts, and posted 29 wins, including 5 shutouts, and 11 losses. With the 29 wins, he was the winningest pitcher in organized baseball in 1953. He had broken the Mountain States League record of Johnny Podres of 27 wins set in Hazard, Kentucky, in 1951. The confidence in his abilities when he told Ken Buckles on June 28th, "I'll win more for you than I'll lose," was demonstrated more than once. Tugerson had accomplished everything except win the pennant. He now had the opportunity to compensate for that shortcoming in the playoffs.

Chapter 9

The Play-Offs

Pankovits had no decision to make about who would open the best-of-five series at Morristown. Everybody knew, including the Red Sox. Tugerson pitched his expected 6-hit game and won by a score of 11-3. But he included a caveat early on. He hit a grand-slam home run in the second inning that gave the Smokies an 8-1 lead. Tugerson was sending a message to the Twins, which Morristown received immediately, that there was a controlled high-speed train headed their way and that they had better get ready. This was the ace's 30th win of the season. The Twins dropped their first game to Kingsport, 10-5.

Buckles started and finished Game 2 and perhaps had his best game of the year, both on the mound and at the plate. The Smokies thumped the Red Sox 15-3. The Smokies' runs came off 22 hits, five of which belonged to Buckles—a triple, a double, and three singles for five RBIs. He allowed eight hits, including two homers which produced the three runs. His pitching and hitting alone were more than enough to handle the Red Sox. Most everybody got in on the scoring act, including Tugerson who played first and went 2-for-6 with an RBI. In Game 2 of the Maryville-Alcoa and Kingsport series, the Twins evened things up by winning an 8-6 decision at Kingsport.

Knoxville lost Game 3 by a score of 16-9. Morristown belted 16 hits, including four homers that produced six runs. Koehnke, who allowed five runs in three innings, started and was charged with the loss. Whitey Diehl relieved Koehnke and relinquished ten runs in 5 1/3 innings. Pankovits pitched the last 2/3 inning just to get it over. The Smokies chalked up a total of six errors in this effort. Tugerson was again at first base while Buckles played left field. Kingsport beat Maryville-Alcoa at home 13-5 and was, like Knoxville, only one game away from the championship series.

Tugerson notched his 31st win in Game 4 to win the series three games to one by a score of 11-5. He allowed seven hits while striking out thirteen and walking only two. Tugerson went 3-for-4 at the plate, knocking in three runs. The Twins, playing at home, evened the series with the Cherokees at two games apiece with a 9-3 win.

The pennant-winning Maryville-Alcoa Twins defeated the Kingsport Cherokees in Game 5 of their series in a rain-shortened 5-inning affair at Hunt Field, 6-5. The Twins led this game 4-0 after the first, fell behind 5-4 after the second, evened the score in the fourth, and won it in the fifth with a homer off the bat of Willie Kirkland.

The Knoxville-Morristown series was played on four consecutive days from August 31st through September 3rd while the Maryville-Alcoa and Kingsport series lasted one day longer. The championship series was set to begin on Saturday, September 5th at the Twins home field.

The Twins won the first game of the championship series over the Smokies in a whimsical meeting that could be labeled anything but a pitching duel. This opening game, played at the Twins' home field, went 10 innings and finally ended after 37 runs had been scored, 19-18. The Smokies had lost by this same score back on August 14th in the fiasco against Big Stone Gap at Chapman Highway Park. This had more than that nightmare with the Braves—more homers, more errors, more freakish plays, more embarrassment. Everybody on the Smokies' staff pitched except Tugerson. Koehnke was charged with the loss. When it was over, everyone on the Smokies roster was glad Tugerson was on their team. He was their only chance.

Game 2 was played the next day, Sunday, on the Smokies' home turf. Of course, Pankovits put the ball and the Smokies' hopes in Tugerson's glove, or more specifically, in his right hand. Tugerson went the distance, notching his 3rd play-off win and his 32nd of the year. The Smokies scored four runs in the opening frame which included a 3-run homer by Charlie Bradford. Games 3 and 4 were scheduled for Tuesday, September 8, 1953, as a home and home twin-bill with the first game set for Hunt Field in Alcoa.

For the first game of this double-header, Pankovits went with Buckles who already had one play-off win to his credit. But it was not Buckles' day. The Twins tagged Buckles for six runs on nine hits in 1 2/3 innings. Relief came in the form of Fred Sarracino who was chased by the Twins in the fourth with three runs. When Bud Koehnke entered the game in the fourth with two out, the Smokies were down 9-6. At the game's end, the Smokies were up 14-11 and Koehnke had pitched one-hit ball. The Smokies' bats put five runs on the board in the top of the ninth. The Smokies were up two games to one as the series moved to Chapman Highway Park for the nightcap.

Was there ever any doubt about who would pitch Game 4? Win or lose Game 3, Pankovits had to give the ball to Tugerson, hopefully, for the last time. Had the Smokies been 1-2 rather than 2-1, Pankovits would still have gone to Tugerson to ensure getting to the championship game. Tugerson was allowed three days' rest between his first and last games in the series with Morristown, but he only had one day's rest between starts in the championship series against the Twins. Exhausted, he had to reach back one last time and bring it home. And he did, in the grandest of styles.

With Knoxville up 5-3 in the bottom of the seventh, Tugerson hit a 2-run homer to finish off the Twins. He circled the bases with a big grin on his face, the first time his teammates had ever seen this. Big Jim had never been one to make light of a batter who had trouble hitting his menacing heater, or a pitcher who gave up a home run to him. But on this day, he simply could not contain himself. He was now a train in full control. The Smokies won by a final score of 8-3. Tugerson scattered 10 hits, struck out seven, and walked three in getting his fourth play-off win and his 33rd of the season. With the last putout, the Smokies mobbed Tugerson, lifted him onto their shoulders and carried him off the field. The Smokies had done what only they knew they could do; they had won the play-offs and had won them convincingly.

The two Knoxville newspapers *The Knoxville Journal* and *The Knoxville News-Sentinel* had made it a practice to inaccurately and sloppily report the efforts of this team, whether they called them the Chapman Park Seviers, the Chapman Park Dark Stars, the Chapman Park Smokies, or the Knoxville Smokies, and the next day's issue of *The Sentinel* was no different. The coverage read, in part, "So elated were the 700 or so spectators that they made up a kitty of about $40 for the big Negro who amassed a 29-11 regular season record." Tugerson's teammates knew that the kitty collected totaled $75 and that Tugerson wanted to share it equally with them. Of course, even though no one took a penny, they knew Tugerson was dead serious. That was his style.

Chapter 10

The Words of Big Jim

The week following Tugerson's 17th win against Morristown at Chapman Highway Park, and only a week before he would win his 20th and then leave for Hot Springs to file the $50,000 lawsuit, he was interviewed by Tom Siler, sportswriter, and later, Sports Editor, for *The Knoxville News-Sentinel.* On July 6, 1953, Siler began his column..."JIM TUGERSON, the Smokies' 17-game winner, is a modest, 26-year-old Negro." (No one, not his teammates, his manager, the team's owner, not even Tom Siler, knew Tugerson's age, one of his most closely-guarded secrets.) Siler continued that the most recent issue of **The Sporting News** listed no pitcher in organized baseball with more wins, pointing out that Tugerson was only one win short having half of the Smokies' 39 wins.

Describing Tugerson as a fast ball pitcher, Siler quoted Tugerson as saying, "I got a change-up, too...and I've been working on a curve. When I get way ahead of a team I try to work on my curve. It breaks about this much—indicating six or seven inches with his fingers—and I know it should be better. But I believe the best thing I do is throw to spots. When I've got my fast ball going where I want it I do pretty well."

Siler reported that Tugerson had been close to signing with the Dodgers, and continued to quote Tugerson, who said, "I've toured with a lot of those teams that barnstorm in the fall...I remember one year—that was after the 1950 season, I think—our team went into Wilmington, Del., to play Robin Roberts' team. I allowed one hit in five innings and struck out 10. Roberts gave up one hit, too."

"Several of the fellows gave me a recommendation.

Campy—Roy Campanella—told the Dodgers about me. Sam Jethroe recommended me to the Braves. Upshot of it all was that I went to Vero Beach with the Dodgers." Tugerson told Siler that the Dodgers were interested and began negotiating with the Clowns for his contract. Tugerson continued, "The Clowns wanted a big price for me. They refused to come down. So the Dodgers lost interest. After all, I can't blame them. Baseball is a gamble and they didn't know that I could make the grade. After I left the Dodgers the Braves asked me to come down to their camp. But I explained the situation. It would have been a waste of time, so I went back to the Clowns."

Tugerson told Siler that he decided after the 1952 season with the Clowns not to return, told them so, and the Clowns eventually agreed to deal him to another club. Tugerson continued, "Campy told me to make the break and get into organized baseball…He told me it would be rough, especially playing in that section; yet, I was willing to sacrifice a better salary to see if I could climb up in the organized leagues." During the time he was working out with Hot Springs, Tugerson met George Earnshaw, a former major league pitcher for nine years who lived in Hot Springs. He told Siler that Earnshaw "….gave me a lot of tips on my pitching, especially on the curve and change-up and I've been working on them as much as possible."

Tugerson suggested that Hot Springs could have optioned him to a higher class of ball than the Class D Mountain States League, but recalled "…I talked to George Earnshaw about it. He told me it would be better to start down in this league and prove myself. I think he was right, too." When Siler asked him if he thought he could win in Class B, Tugerson replied, "I think so, but I don't know. I'm sure I'm fast enough. I've pitched good ball against big leaguers, and I won with the Clowns. But I've got to improve my curve ball. I'm not kidding myself. Then, too, when you talk about winning you know it depends a lot on the team you're with."

Siler pointed out that Tugerson had obviously been the workhorse for the Smokies, frequently pitching with only two days rest or working in relief. Suggesting that he was overworked, Tugerson responded, "Naw, I don't think I'm overworked. I like to pitch. And I stay in shape. I eat a little snack of eggs and milk after the night games, then go to bed. I sleep almost all day, don't play around none. No, don't drink, not even a beer." Tugerson told Siler that after the barnstorming tours are over in the fall, he lives with his family in Winter Haven, Florida, and cooks in a restaurant in the off season.

Years later when Tugerson was a shift lieutenant with the Winter Haven Police Department, in an article titled **"Former Pitcher In A League By Himself,"** in *The Lakeland Ledger,* Tugerson reminisced about his baseball career. He talked about pitching for the Bartow All-Stars and beating both the Kansas City Monarchs and the Clowns. Both these teams asked him to join them, but he was hesitant to go on the road, pointing out he could stay home and cook at the Sundown Restaurant and get $50 a game for playing once a week. The Homestead Grays, the dominant Negro League team, offered him a contract, but he opted instead to sign with the Monarchs. His stay with the Monarchs was short-lived as he got a sore arm overthrowing in an effort to impress Buck O'Neil, the Monarch's manager. He then signed with the Clowns, joining his brother, Leander, and played the 1951 and 1952 seasons there.

Tugerson also spoke of his time with the Clowns and his rooming with future Hall of Famer Hank Aaron. "He was my roommate when we were with the Clowns. He left the Clowns and went to Indianapolis in the Braves farm system. When he came to camp, all he had was a li'l bitty handbag with his glove and shoes and clothes and everything. Both of us being rookies, and neither of us drink and both of us spend most of the time in our rooms, so they put us together. We had fun. It was wholesome and clean fun, we just didn't drink. And we didn't believe in staying out late. We rapped the ball, and then we'd go home."

Tugerson talked about the pressure he felt from both the Cotton States League following the forfeited game at Hot Springs and from the owner of the Clowns (Syd Pollock) to rejoin the Clowns rather than return to Knoxville. He also addressed the reason he returned to Knoxville rather than rejoining the Clowns. Tugerson said, "It would have defeated the purpose. See, if I had a contract there and broke it, I would have denied the right of Negro players to play in the league at any time. That wouldn't have helped the black people, baseball or nothin'."

Tugerson confirmed during this interview with *The Ledger* late in his life what the newspapers had reported in 1953—his promise the night of the forfeiture to sue the Cotton States League. Following his return to Knoxville after filing the lawsuit, there was little talk of the lawsuit among his teammates, and Tugerson only voluntarily spoke of it once. Shortly after returning to the team, a few members of the pitching staff, including Koehnke, Buckles, and Diehl, heard Tugerson's own words about it. These pitchers, as well as their other Smokies teammates, were awed by Tugerson. He was such a private man, and they had such respect for him that they were always reluctant to tread on his private turf—his inner sanctum. This one occasion was an exception.

Koehnke, with his head bowed and not looking at Jim, asked him if he thought he had a chance of winning the lawsuit. Tugerson replied that he knew there was no chance of winning but that it was something he had to do even though he knew it might ruin his chances of attaining his goal of playing in the major leagues. He felt that it might make it easier for those who followed. Tugerson expressed his view to his fellow pitchers how unfair he thought it was not to allow him to pitch because he was a Negro. He pointed out that a Cuban pitcher on the Bathers was actually darker than him, but no one ever said anything about his playing for the Bathers.

Tugerson may have found some slight consolation, if he knew it, that the Cubans were as puzzled as he about the difference drawn between acceptance of the Cuban players and not the Negroes. In George Stone's book, **"Muscle"** the playing manager of the Kingsport club, Leo "Muscle" Shoals, talked about how the Cuban players never understood why the Negroes were never allowed to eat and sleep with the team the same as them. The Cubans also thought it was unfair and the distinction never made sense to them. Muscle also told the story of how Knoxville's Regas Restaurant allowed his Kingsport team—whites, Cubans, and Negroes—to eat in one of the two back meeting rooms on weeknights when the restaurant was not full.

I'm familiar with the rooms Muscle described at Regas, having eaten in all the rooms at Regas over the past 45 years. One of those rooms has an emergency exit into the alley. Unfortunately, most of the players on the 1953 Smokies team, black or white, could not have afforded to eat at Regas.

My dad sold his restaurant in 1957 when public eating places were still segregated. I know from first-hand experience, however, that integration was not carte blanche with the passage of the Civil Rights Act of 1964. In 1966, I attended my first 2-week summer camp with the Army National Guard at Fort Stewart, Georgia. As a member of the supply unit, I violated the cardinal rule of military service (never volunteer for anything) and raised my hand to be part of the clean-up and lock-up detail upon departure. What this meant was we made sure that everything got loaded, and that the buildings were secured. But, more importantly, what this also meant was the detail had at its disposal two "deuce and a halfs" to haul the supplies and personnel, neither of which were required to catch up to and join the convoy en route back to Knoxville. That meant we could stop and eat anything, anywhere, anytime, or so we thought. We were civilians again, but still in uniform.

Because it was convenient we pulled into a truck stop in a somewhat desolate stretch of road in South Georgia for lunch. We went in and seated ourselves at a big round table large enough to accommodate all of us. After a few minutes, a waitress came to the table with her order pad but told us she couldn't serve the Negro with us. This black guardsman, who was popular and well-liked by all because of his wit, got up and offered to go back to the trucks, saying we could bring him something. We all rose in unison and left. I can still see the faces of the truck stop patrons as we left.

Forty-two years later, Ken Buckles told me about Jim referring to fans at Harlan, Kentucky as "the little people." I knew what he meant. I had already seen their faces.

Big Jim

Chapter 11

The Eyes of Teammate Ken Buckles

Fifty-four and a half years after seeing Ken Buckles in a Smokies uniform at Chapman Park, I would talk to him for the first time by phone after tracking him down through the Internet. We would immediately connect and swap stories for over an hour. He would tell me that he has Parkinson's disease and cancer which had metastasized and that his life-long friend, Whitey Diehl, now lives in Sebastopol, California and is having trouble getting around. He knew, of course, that Tugerson was dead, but did not know any details until I told him. I also told him Tugerson's age in 1953 which Tugerson never revealed. I would tell Ken that I had spoken to Art Sabulsky earlier the same day and had determined that Art, now 77, is under constant care. I spoke briefly to Art and determined he was not alert enough to carry on a conversation. His care-giver told me Art still had clippings from his baseball days. I also determined that Art, a widower, was a retired Allegheny County, Pennsylvania police detective and living in Harwick, Pennsylvania. Ken, saddened to hear of Art's condition, would recall that Art was a good outfielder. He was also saddened to hear that Vince Pankovits had passed away in February 2007 in Richmond at age 87.

Ten days later I would travel to Bettendorf, Iowa, where I would meet and talk to Ken Buckles in person. Very soon after personally meeting Ken I would see short bios of Tugerson, Pankovits, Diehl, and himself that he had penned several years after the 1953 season. His description of Tugerson, which I found to be particularly poignant and insightful, reads, *"a tall, husky black pitcher of uncertain age who won 33 games for the Knoxville Smokies in 1953, more than anyone else in all of professional baseball..."D"*

Big Jim

Chapter 11

The Eyes of Teammate Ken Buckles

Fifty-four and a half years after seeing Ken Buckles in a Smokies uniform at Chapman Park, I would talk to him for the first time by phone after tracking him down through the Internet. We would immediately connect and swap stories for over an hour. He would tell me that he has Parkinson's disease and cancer which had metastasized and that his life-long friend, Whitey Diehl, now lives in Sebastopol, California and is having trouble getting around. He knew, of course, that Tugerson was dead, but did not know any details until I told him. I also told him Tugerson's age in 1953 which Tugerson never revealed. I would tell Ken that I had spoken to Art Sabulsky earlier the same day and had determined that Art, now 77, is under constant care. I spoke briefly to Art and determined he was not alert enough to carry on a conversation. His care-giver told me Art still had clippings from his baseball days. I also determined that Art, a widower, was a retired Allegheny County, Pennsylvania police detective and living in Harwick, Pennsylvania. Ken, saddened to hear of Art's condition, would recall that Art was a good outfielder. He was also saddened to hear that Vince Pankovits had passed away in February 2007 in Richmond at age 87.

Ten days later I would travel to Bettendorf, Iowa, where I would meet and talk to Ken Buckles in person. Very soon after personally meeting Ken I would see short bios of Tugerson, Pankovits, Diehl, and himself that he had penned several years after the 1953 season. His description of Tugerson, which I found to be particularly poignant and insightful, reads, *"a tall, husky black pitcher of uncertain age who won 33 games for the Knoxville Smokies in 1953, more than anyone else in all of professional baseball..."D"* *leagues to the Bigs. Jim had played in the Negro Leagues for a few years and with the breaking of the color line had become the property of the Hot Springs Bathers of the Class "C" Cotton States League. Unfortunately for Jim but a God-send for us, he was not allowed to pitch there because of the color of his skin. Eventually, he filed a $50,000 law suit against the league for violating his civil rights...a suit he knew he couldn't win, given the social climate of 1953 in Arkansas...three tempestuous years before Dwight Eisenhower out-flanked Arkansas Governor Orval Faubus and started the integration of Little Rock public schools.*

A soft-spoken, philosophical but very private man with a wry sense of humor and a wicked sinking side-armed fastball he could thread a needle with, he let the bigotry that cascaded down upon him just roll off his broad back. A MAN, if ever one walked this earth."

Ken's short narrative of Pankovits that follows reads a bit different: *"Our playing manager. Vince to his face... Pan-KO-eetz, with hard emphasis on the middle syllable...among his players, never skip or skipper. An intense, driven, combative, foul-mouthed, uncompromising. bull-headed man with the overall appearance of a Cosa Nostra hit-man. A catcher, he gave no quarter and expected none. In his early thirties, Vince set the tone on the field for his team and although we fought with him and argued with...almost always to no avail...he was the unquestioned leader of our sorry team in this sorrier league."*

Ken liked Pankovits and thought he was a good manager with a tough job. Whitey Diehl and Pankovits did not get along at all. It finally got so bad after a heated argument over Pankovits pulling Whitey and making a pitching change that Ken had to serve as the communications intermediary as Whitey and Pankovits would not talk to each other.

Now Ken's bio of Bob "Whitey" Diehl *"...best friend, even though their (Diehl and Buckles) outlooks on almost any aspect of life were polar opposites. A 6'5", 215 pound ex-high school athletic adversary of (Buckles), they later became basketball teammates at the University of Iowa. Whitey, at 21, was a good-looking guy. Very active socially in his college fraternity, he had a classic, John Barrymore Roman-nosed profile topped by wavy, blonde hair; good manners when he chose to use them and a way with the ladies. To Whitey's way of thinking...which therefore was the only way anyone could possibly think...there was nothing he could not do better than anyone else. Seldom true and very rarely acknowledged."*

And finally, Ken's succinct autobio, *"...20 years old; an unsophisticated, naïve, highly emotional, very modestly-talented first-year pitcher in the Cincinnati Reds minor-league system. Brash, intensely competitive, unfailingly hard on himself. Came into this league determined to quickly scale the ladder to the major leagues, although in his heart he doubted his own abilities...regardless of what some Cincinnati scout had told him. 6'3" tall, 165 stringy pounds, curly brown hair, bright, eager brown eyes. Baseball was serious...the rest of life was fun. Known to brood on occasion."*

I would be able to locate only two other living member of the 1953 Smokies—David "Pepsi" Mobley, a native of Lancaster, South Carolina, found living in Charlotte, North Carolina, and David "Red" Clapp –a life long-resident of Corryton, a community in Knox County north of Knoxville.

The following recollections and experiences are those of Ken Buckles that I have selectively carved from his writings of over 30 years ago and re-written. Ken wrote three versions of that 1953 season with the Smokies. The first version was factual and entirely non-fiction whereas the second and third became more and more fictionalized. The following events and stories were extracted from the original version only.

"Our ace was a tall, tireless black sidearmer named Jim Tugerson....And Jim had to be one of the nicest guys I've every met, along with being one helluva pitcher. I'm not sure how old Jim was at the time…could've been anywhere from 25 to 40…but he could do it. He threw sidearm and was the only righthanded sidearmer I ever saw who backed lefthanders out of the batters box. He was a cook in Florida in the wintertime, and he just went about his business, which consisted of winning 33 games (counting the playoffs) and losing 11. He pitched 330 innings, which was 100 more than anyone else in the league, and he led the league in shutouts with 5 and in strikeouts with 286. He played 10 games at first after Forbes left and hit .308 with 35 RBIs for the year. He was active.

Other than the ballpark, we never saw Jim. He could not room in the same hotels we stayed at on the road, and I have no idea where he lived in Knoxville. Black guys in the big leagues who played later on should get down on their knees and thank the Lord for guys like Jim Tugerson and the other black guys who played baseball in the 1940's and 1950's South. Guys like Tugerson labored and took malicious abuse in obscurity…for peanuts. Discrimination and outright bigotry was a way of life in the towns in the Mountain States League then, and it was heaped on the blacks in that league. There were no 'advisors' to help them…no one to 'protect' them from uncomfortable or downright untenable situations. They were on their own, and it was hard."

Ken Buckles penned those words over 20 years after celebrating that play-off win over the Maryville-Alcoa Twins in early September, 1953. He would never see Tugerson again after that day, or for that matter, any of his Smokies teammates other than Bob "Whitey" Diehl. Another 35 years later, Buckles furnished me all the words he had written in hopes that what he experienced that summer in the Tennessee, Virginia, and Kentucky towns making up the Mountain States League, would be told. That summer was special for him because that team, led by an extraordinary man and ball player, overcame almost overwhelming odds and obstacles in achieving that unlikely victory over the

Twins, a victory that may very well have been the sweetest of his life.

Buckles, the third winningest pitcher on the Smokies' staff that year, went 9 and 6 during the regular season, pitching 132 innings with an ERA of 4.09. He also won Game 2 of the play-offs against Morristown, perhaps his best outing of the year, helping the Smokies get into the finals against the Twins.

Buckles attended a Cincinnati Reds tryout camp at Burlington, Iowa, during the summer of 1952 but did not sign until a year later when he still had a year of basketball eligibility left at Iowa. In the spring of '53 he attended a Reds minor league training camp at Jackson, Tennessee, for a couple of weeks, then returned to Iowa to finish the semester. The Reds called and told him to report to the Burlington Bees of the Class B Three I League managed by the legendary Johnny Vander Meer, a big league pitcher for 13 years whose record of back-to-back no-hitters in June, 1938, still stands. Soon after arriving, Whitey Diehl signed with the Reds and showed up at Burlington. Whitey had pitched three years at Iowa and was a pretty fair pitcher.

Unfortunately for both Ken and Whitey, Vander Meer had continued to pitch after leaving the major leagues, and had, in fact, pitched a no-hitter in 1952 while pitching for Tulsa in the Texas League. Vander Meer considered himself the most effective reliever at Burlington so Ken and Whitey languished in the bullpen. After relative inactivity for several weeks, the Reds gave both of them train tickets to Knoxville and told them to report immediately to the Knoxville Smokies of the Class D Mountain States League.

What was a town the size of Knoxville doing playing in a Class D league? And why, according to the Sporting News they read on the train, were they playing under .500 ball? Why was Knoxville not in the Sally League or the Southern Association? What they also did not know was that those were sentiments of the owner of the Knoxville

Smokies, Dr. Grubb, who wanted nothing more than that, and who was just trying to keep things together until he could do just that the following year.

Their instructions were to report to the Smokies' manager, Vince Pankovits, at the Parkway Hotel, which, as it turned out was located 3-4 miles south of downtown Knoxville on Chapman Highway. Their first meeting with Pankovits did not go well. He initially insisted that they stay at the Parkway where the rest of the team, except for the black players, stayed when "at home." Both resisted Pankovits' demand, telling him they were big boys and were accustomed to having their own place. Besides finding a suitable apartment complete with a fireplace and French doors that opened out onto a roof porch, they also bought a 1942 Dodge to ferry their carcasses back and forth between their downtown apartment and the Parkway.

Neither Buckles nor Diehl dressed the first night they were there (June 19) but rather sat in the right field bleachers, normally reserved for the black fans. They also noticed the drinking fountain had a sign over it, "Whites Only," and the garden hose was used by the blacks. They watched a pitcher they would come to know well, Larry Koehnke, nail several Norton batters between the shoulder blades on a somewhat regular basis. They would come to know that Koehnke's control was at its best when he was throwing at the batter as opposed to the strike zone. The Smokies beat Norton 9-8.

After the game they went to the dressing room and met the team and, of course, ran into Pankovits again who was not happy when told they had found a place to live. It was then he laid down the "call in every morning at 7:00 rule" so that they wouldn't be lying in bed all day. They took turns calling. One would climb out of bed, put their pants on, and then go across the street to the Cities gas station to call Vince. When he answered, they'd simply say, "We're up, Vince," and hang up. Then the one that called would go back to bed. Vince knew what they were doing, but it did not matter. The rule stayed in force until they moved into the Parkway near the season's end. Pankovits and Whitey never got along, not from the beginning. Pankovits was a pretty good manager and adequate catcher but his greatest attribute was his fierce competiveness. Vince was an "in your face" type competitor, a fighter, and was admired for that.

The ball park was located several miles out of Knoxville on Chapman Highway, "out in the boonies" where there wasn't anybody or anything—nothing. Calling themselves the "Knoxville" Smokies was a misnomer and confusing. No one in Knoxville knew who the Smokies were or where the ball park was located.

On the Road at Pennington Gap

Pennington Gap, Virginia was the Smokies' home away from home for a couple of reasons. First, and foremost, Vince Pankovits' wife was there. That was where they lived. Secondly, Pennington Gap was conveniently located to all the Virginia and Kentucky clubs in the league—Big Stone Gap, Norton, Harlan, and Middlesboro—as well as Kingsport on the Tennessee side. While Vince was with his wife, the rest of this team, except for the black players, was holed up at the Pennington Gap Hotel, which was the absolute pits. There was no fire escape. Each room had a knotted rope tied around the radiator to be thrown out the window and used as a rope ladder in the event the place went up in smoke. This rope was a feature of every room except the room used by Diehl and Buckles. Their room had no rope fire escape because it had no windows. The hotel was, without question, the worst any on the team had ever encountered.

The hotel had a restaurant that served hominy with every meal, a Southern delicacy, but not a staple on the plates of Iowa college boys. They had never eaten hominy and never would again. But for between 60 and 85 cents they could get pretty full, which was not bad considering meal money in this league was $2.00 per day. Such things were important when pulling down a whopping $225 a month gross.

There wasn't much else to do in Pennington Gap. The movie theater was only open at night when the team was playing, and the local pool hall had one table where all the locals lined up to play. About the only entertainment left was staying at the hotel playing cards and listening to the Davis Sisters' singing their big hit, "I Forgot More Than You'll Ever Know About Him." That song was played all season on every radio station and juke box in every town traveled.

The ball park at Big Stone Gap has to be where the term "sublime and ridiculous" originated. First the ridiculous. The dressing room had either been dug out of the earth or was in a cave. The walls consisted of embedded railroad crossties. There were nails in the crossties on which to hang clothes and a couple of benches to sit on while changing. The floors were dirt, including the shower area, but someone had placed wooden pallets on the shower floor. There was no where for the water to actually drain; it just eventually soaked into the ground. At least the pallets would keep you out of the mud for a while. When three or four guys got in the shower at the same time, the water got pretty deep, and you'd have to slosh around in the muddy water while trying to wash everything else.

Now the sublime. The ball park, peculiarly shaped because of the unforgiving terrain, being dug out in that mountain seemed almost irreverent. It was 330 down the lines but was only 300 straight-away center field. The beauty surrounding the ball field, the greenery, the coolness of the evening, the clean mountain air, deserved better than the cracks of bats and infield chatter. With that backdrop it became clear why the people who lived there stayed. It really didn't matter that there wasn't anything to do. Just living there was enough.

Buckles' First Wins

Aside from the scenery, Buckles had another reason for being partial to Big Stone Gap. A week after his first win slipped away against Kingsport and ended with Tugerson's declaration, "I'll win more for you than I'll lose," Buckles would finally get to savor his first win—at Big Stone Gap. This time, he went all the way and needed no relief help from Tugerson or anyone else. He gave up ten hits but contributed two singles in the 10-5 victory.

Buckles' second win came only three days later at Middlesboro. He developed a fondness for Middlesboro as well, but not because of its beauty. The ball park, rather than being carved out of a mountain, had previously been a stock car race track. The second win had been made sweeter than the first because he belted a two-run homer to help his cause. Whitey Diehl had started the game but was pounded for five hits and five runs in the first without getting an out. Buckles had repeatedly told Whitey that he was "aiming" the ball, and as a result, was taking something off of it. Whitey did not like being repeatedly told anything, and he repeatedly denied that he was aiming the ball.

After Jim Williams struggled through 4 1/3 innings, giving up four more hits and as many runs, Buckles came in and pitched hitless ball the rest of the way. And, oh yeah, he blasted his two-run homer in the eighth to tie the score at 9-9. Unbelievable. This from a guy who hit .235 in high school and .280 in semi-pro. He gave it the full home run trot as if this was an every day event, shook hands, the whole deal. He got them out in the 8th and 9th, and his teammates got three more runs. Buckles would years later admit this win was as big a thrill as he ever got in sports.

The Cave

As it turned out, there was a little more entertainment in Middlesboro than Big Stone Gap. The Middlesboro centerfielder tipped Buckles about a night spot called "The Cave." Buckles' win was the last game in the series, and they were returning to Knoxville that night but decided to check out this joint anyway. Buckles and Diehl were riding with Bill Forbes and Bobby Grose, who always ran together, in Forbes' car, a 1951 Pontiac. This was one of three cars that the team normally used to travel to games, the other two being Lindley's 1952 Buick and Pankovits'1952 Chrysler. The drivers were paid gas money. There was no team bus.

The cave, which was on the second floor of some building, had no sign, lobby, vestibule, or anything, just through the door and wham—poker tables, a long bar to the right, and two blackjack tables in the back of the room. There were no women in the place, only men, and they were all gambling with silver dollars. After watching for a while, Buckles and Diehl slid into a couple of the blackjack seats and got $5 worth of silver dollars each. Whitey was tapped out in short order. Buckles won initially but lost to the house due to the quick hands of the dealer. He got away from the table with a dollar and bought a bottle of wine to enjoy on the trip back to Knoxville. Both were broke. They met Forbes and Grose for the trip back. The two other riders in Forbes' car had opted to return to Knoxville with Lindley and Pankovits, an option they now realized they should have taken.

Forbes and Grose were an interesting pair. They were defined as "veterans" in D ball parlance which meant they had at least three years' experience in professional baseball. Each Class D minor league team was allowed four veterans, six limited service players, and the rest rookies. Forbes, a native of Cleveland, Ohio, and Grose, a native of Dallas, Pennsylvania, had been around the low minors for several years and knew they were not going anywhere. As a result they pretty much did as they pleased. There were not many rules, but what few there were, Forbes and Grose broke. Both enjoyed drinking and chasing women.

Signs and Pankovits

Everybody in the league had the Smokies' signs. This was because only Pankovits gave them without relay to the third base coach, without indicators or decoys, just zap— Vince to the hitter and base runner. He did not go to his cap, then to the letters, then to the belt, and back to the cap. Nothing like that. Just a straight sign to the hitter and runner. No covert communication. The other teams' pitchers and catchers looked at Vince to know what to throw. Pankovits did not buy it. No one had his signs.

Buckles recalled the matter came to a head in Norton when he got on first and was having trouble seeing Vince to get the sign. Norton's first baseman and playing manager, Walt Dixon, who was always neck-and-neck with Muscle Shoals of Kingsport for the hitting title, told Buckles he would relay Pankovits' sign to him, that he had a clear view of Pankovits. Dixon volunteered to tell him if Pankovits put something on. When the top of the inning was over and Buckles was grabbing his glove to return to the mound, he told Pankovits that Dixon was picking up the signs. Pankovits still resisted.

But it was not just the offensive signs that had been compromised. It was the signs Pankovits gave to his pitcher behind the plate as well. Most catchers used one finger to signal fast ball, two for a curve. Pankovits signaled fast ball with his fist, curve ball by tapping his four fingers against his thigh. When he signaled fast ball, his elbow was in next to his torso. When he signaled curve, his elbow was away from his torso. Elbow in, fast ball. Elbow out, curve ball. The opposing third base coaches had come up with verbal signals to let the batter know what was coming. Everyone knew except Pankovits.

When Buckles returned to the mound, he threw the opposite of Pankovits' signals. When he threw a curve, the batter was hitting the dirt. When he threw the fast ball, the batter was leaning looking for curve and would get caught looking. Vince comes out and admits Buckles was right. From that point forward, Pankovits switched signs every inning from then through the play-offs. He changed all the signs—the pitches, hit and take, all of them. And it made a big difference.

After the game Pankovits cornered Buckles in private and again told Buckles he was right about the signs but cautioned him to never talk to him or show him up like that again in front of the team. Pankovits emphasized all Buckles had to do was sit down and talk to him. Buckles knew better. Polite conversation didn't work with Pankovits. That was mid-July and Norton ended the Smokies' 11-game win streak that night, but no one knew the signs the rest of the season.

Joke on Freddie Sarracino

With 34 games left to play Tugerson won his 23rd at home against Middlesboro, 11-4. Only in the Class D Mountain States League would a pitcher have the opportunity to win 30 that year. Only in this bush league would something that great happen. Of course, on the night of this Tugerson win, another thing happened in this bush league that was pretty unbelievable as well.

Freddie Sarracino, a 17-year-old kid just out of high school a couple of months, came to Knoxville about the same time as Buckles and Diehl. Baltimore had paid him a $3,000 bonus to sign, and no one had yet figured out what prompted the Orioles to make that donation. Sarracino had a penchant to doze off in the dugout every game at about the time the home team was taking the field. He'd pull his cap down, lean up against the wall of the dugout, and using his glove as a pillow, start sawing some logs. No one really cared but Pankovits on this night recognized the stage could be easily set to pull one off on Freddie.

Vince set it up with Ben Pardue, the Middlesboro manager; with Gordon Wood, the Middlesboro lead-off batter; with both umpires; and, of course, with Tugerson. Lastly, Vince set it up with his bench, the pitchers and reserves. Then it's game time, and the players run out onto the field. As usual, the cap came down, the glove was put in place, and Sarracino was gone.

Tugerson wound up and threw the first pitch right down the middle. "Ball," said the umpire. Pankovits turned around to the ump; he could not believe it. Tugerson was leaning on his knees and staring in disbelief. The ump told Pankovits to get back down. Freddie continued to snooze. Tugerson went into his wind-up and brought it home again, right in there. The ump said, "Ball two." Pankovits went crazy and Tugerson tossed his glove in the air to express his disagreement and disgust. The ump took a few steps toward the Smokies' dugout and peered.

This umpire, reportedly the brother of either Homer or Jethro of the popular country act of the '50's, was a pretty good actor himself. This, coupled with the fact he had only one good eye (the other being glass) made this gag perfect. He was considered, however, one of the best umpires in the league. Finally, Tugerson wound up and threw the third pitch with the same result. Pankovits tossed his mask, Tugerson threw up his hands, and the dugout was screaming at the guy and throwing towels out of the dugout. Freddie still had not budged.

The home plate ump stalked to the edge of the dugout and announced, "Okay, Sarracino, you're out of here. Get out of here." Freddie started coming to life, stuttering inaudibly, and the umpire then said, "That'll cost you fifty dollars, Sarracino...Don't give me any of your crap. Now get out of here." He waved his mask toward the dugout, gesturing with it to get Sarracino moving. Freddie questioned the fifty dollars, trying to make some sense out of what had just happened when the ump says, "That's fifty more...every word you say will be fifty more. Now get out of here."

Buckles and Diehl consoled Freddie, told him to shut up, and then helped him out of the dugout, around the corner, and into the locker room where Freddie tried to find out what had just happened. Diehl convinced Freddie that he had yelled at the umpire "that he was blind in one eye and couldn't see out of the other." Whitey told him that the umpire really was blind in one eye and apparently was upset and hurt by Sarracino's comments. Ragging an umpire was one thing, Whitey explained, but getting on him about personal afflictions is something else again. Whitey continued to lay it on pretty thick and finally Freddie agreed to apologize to the umpire after the game.

After the game Buckles, Diehl, and Pankovits accompanied Sarracino to the umpire's dressing room. Sarracino knocked and when the umpire appeared, Pankovits, like an embarrassed parent, coaxed Sarracino, and told the umpire, "Freddie has something he wants to say. Don't you, Freddie?" Freddie stepped forward and apologized for saying what Whitey had told him he had said. The umpire told Freddie he'd better learn to watch his mouth, said that the fine stood, and slammed the door.

Sarracino waited a couple of weeks for the letter to come down from the league office about his fine, but it never came. Vince continued to lead him on, explaining to him that on fines over $50, the player's parent club was notified and any further action would have to come from there, in this case, Baltimore. No one ever told Sarracino anything differently. This incident had little effect on Freddie. After a week or so, he started drifting off again, albeit not as soundly.

Repo Man Raided Ball Park, Took Uniforms

On August 13 the team got in from Kingsport around 2:00 a.m., got some sleep, and then got to the ball park at about 5:30 p.m. as always. When Buckles and Diehl walked into the dressing room there were eight or nine guys standing there in sliding pads and sanitary socks, but no uniforms. Bats were piled on the floor and balls were everywhere. Outside, home plate and the pitching rubber had been pulled up and were gone. Light bulbs were missing from the light poles. Pankovits showed up and after talking to Dr. Grubb, he told everyone what they already knew. The finance company had repossessed everything it could lay its hands on—the uniforms, home plate, the pitching rubber, light bulbs, scoreboard numerals, the bat and ball bags. Grubb told Pankovits he owned a one-third interest in a sporting goods store (which, according to Red Clapp was Tennessee Sporting Goods on Magnolia Avenue in Knoxville), and that he could replace everything that had been taken, including the uniforms. So everyone just sat and waited until the uniforms and stuff showed up.

The uniforms arrived but were not in the same class as the Smokies' uniforms they had been wearing. These new "unies," straight from the sporting goods store, were white with red piping and little collars on the back of the neck like the unies of 25 years before. There was nothing on the front or back of the shirts, no name, numbers, nothing. Slick. The socks were heavy ribbed cotton, bright red with a bunch of thick white stripes on them and white stirrups, cut so low they sank into the shoes. The replacement unies were too small on everyone, and the caps shrank the first time they got wet. *(I have a snap shot of several Smokies in the dugout wearing these uniforms, and they remind me of those worn by the New York Knights in the movie, "The Natural." I've also seen a photo of the 1934 Smokies and they also appear very similar. Unfortunately, I have seen Jim Tugerson wearing this uniform in a photo taken by noted Negro*

Leagues photographer Ernest C. Withers of Roy Campanella's 1953 barnstorming team which includes 15 ball players, all major leaguers except three, including Tugerson. In this photo which is posted on the Minot Mallard's web site, Tugerson is wearing a pitching jacket to hide this uniform, which he had when he left Knoxville, and I suspect, to conceal his embarrassment as well.)

Most teams would have been too embarrassed and mad to wear these unies but not Knoxville. The team made a joke of it the same way their opponents did. Bobby Grose, the team's practical joker, using a marking pen wrote "6 7/8," his hat size, on the back of his uniform. It caught on and pretty soon "7 1/8" and "6 5/8" and the like were turning up everywhere. Then block "K's" started appearing on the fronts. The Smokies wore these uniforms every game from then through the play-offs, and they carried the bats loose and the balls in sanitary socks. Strange as it seemed, that craziness made the team play better the rest of the year and inspired it to really make a run at league-leading Maryville-Alcoa.

Bobby Grose, the Jokester

Grose, as just noted in the unies story, was the team jokester. Grose, like everyone else on the team except Tugerson, smoked. But he never left the bench to grab a smoke the way everyone else did. He would stay in the dugout with his cigarette cupped in his hand. When he took a drag, he'd cover his face with his cap and blow the smoke through the little vent holes.

Grose was also the first guy on the team to see the movie "Shane," which opened that summer in Knoxville. Grose, like the rest of the team, saw that flick 3-4 times that summer. Grose was really taken with "Shane," particularly Jack Palance's character, Wilson. Grose especially liked Palance's line, "Prove It," which got Wilson killed when he said it to Shane. Grose would walk around the dressing room, abscond with a teammate's personal belonging and when challenged would say, "Prove it."

Grose was so taken with Wilson that he bought a squirt gun. He would wait until a runner reached first, which required that the umpire reposition himself in front of second base, presenting Grose with the opportunity to squirt the back of the umpire's neck. The umpire would swat his neck and look around and there would be Grose patting his glove and silently mouthing "Prove it." He kept it up for a couple of weeks, squirting umpires, the bench, opposing first basemen when he took his lead. He got caught several times by the umpires, and they would tell him to knock it off, but he never got tossed for doing it. Several squirt guns were seized, but he'd just buy another and go at it again. Grose was a funny guy.

The Dick Carney Story as Recollected by Whitey Diehl

Dick Carney came to the club in mid-July from Harlan, having been traded for Jack Jones, the third baseman. He played the last 44 games plus the play-offs. He was a little guy, 5'7," stocky, and a scooter. He had great hands and for his size had great power. He always seemed to make plays at critical times. He made a big difference in the club's winning percentage down the stretch.

Carney used to sit in the dressing room before games and peel dead skin off his feet. When asked how his feet got so mangy, he would say that they got frostbitten in Korea, and an appropriate counter response would be made making a mockery of his story. Everyone wrote off what he said about his feet as a good story. He seemed to get annoyed that no one believed him but then he was very temperamental and moody. [When Carney later related a "war story" about his time in Korea, both Buckles and Diehl questioned his tale and poked fun. According to Buckles, Diehl was so "guilt ridden, it was pitiful". Because Diehl was so affected by Carney's story, I asked him in March, 2008 to email me his recollections of the Carney story. That verbatim account follows.]

On the ride home from an away game, perhaps Harlan, Kentucky the conversation in the car somehow stumbled into war stories. There were stories of combat that the individual storyteller had heard from a friend, relative, or other sources. Each succeeding story was told with the solemnity and enthusiasm of a first-hand account. The only player who told no stories was Dick Carney. He seemed to grow more quiet and surly as the miles passed. Finally, he blurted out, "Shut up! Why don't you all just shut up? None of you know anything about what it's like to fight a battle, so why don't you just shut up?"

I responded, "Well, Dick, I suppose you know all about it. Come on tell us how it really is. You know so much about it, tell us a good one." Carney just looked at me with disdain written all over his face. He went back to being quiet and brooding. The other guys, having been equally rebuffed, began to taunt him. Finally he said, "All right, I'll tell you a story. I'll tell you what it is like."

"I was with the Marines on the Inchon Peninsula in the Korean conflict. We had worked our way up the Yaloo River on a mission when we suddenly found ourselves in a trap. The Chinese had moved machine guns onto the bluffs overlooking the river. Every time we raised our heads above the snow banks, we were greeted with a burst of gunfire. We were completely exposed. The only way out was to cross the frozen Yaloo, but it was early spring and the river had begun to thaw."

"The word came down for my squad, of which I was the leader, to cross the river and then direct fire at the enemy while the next group scampered across. We took off with 50 caliber bullets kicking up the snow all around us, onto the icy river, running as fast as we could. Suddenly the ice cracked, chasms broke open, men plunged into the icy water. Because I was the first to go, I was closer to the shore when I went in, I broke through the thinning shoreline ice and made it to the other side. The others drowned or were shot."

"The Marines moved further up the valley where the ice would be thicker, but also closer to the enemy guns. As the next group started across, I rose up and sprayed the ridges with gunfire. The Chinese turned their attention to me which was just enough of a diversion for a few more Marines to make it across. They did what I did until finally we silenced their guns and were able to escape before the Chinese got reinforcements."

"I spent two years in and out of hospitals suffering from frostbite. At one point the medics were going to amputate both legs. I lost all my teeth—frozen. I thought my nose was going to rot away. It was a terrifying experience. It still is. I have nightmares. So why don't you all just shut up. I don't want to hear any more war stories."

We all kind of guffawed, not really believing his story, because he wasn't typically believable. "Great story, Dick. You topped us all." Guffaw. Guffaw.

About a month later I was at the Parkway Hotel waiting to go to the ball park. I picked up either The Saturday Evening Post or Look magazine. On the inside of the cover the bold print said, "Dick Carney, winner of the Silver Star for meritorious service..."

I dropped the magazine, looked across the lobby at Carney, and felt absolutely, ashamedly embarrassed. I walked across the lobby and with great humility offered the most sincere apology I have ever extended anyone.

Harlan

Tugerson was scheduled to pitch the first game of a 2-game series at Harlan the last week of the season. As the sun was setting, Tugerson went down the left field line a little to start warming up. Several players including Buckles, Diehl, Rengers, and Sabulsky were standing next to the dugout, just relaxing and talking. The stands running down the left field line began to fill, and the fans were vocal and foul-mouthed. The line each way had a ten foot high chain link fence that ran several feet past first and third. This served to protect the players from the fans, and the fans from the players.

The fans along the third base side started to really get on Tugerson. What more could they have asked for? A visiting team, a black pitcher, and a ten foot high chain link fence to hide behind.

One of them yells "Hey nigger. Hey nigger. Hey…answer me, you fuckin' nigger." Tugerson just kept warming up, getting loose, didn't look up or change expression.

"You think you're too good to answer me, black ass?" A few laugh and toss a couple more winners.

Being from Iowa, Buckles and Diehl had never heard this kind of verbal abuse toward anyone. In fact, all of the 1953 Smokies, except Red Clapp and Charlie Bradford, were from somewhere other than the South. The fans continued throwing racial jabs and Big Jim continued throwing the baseball.

"Why don't you go on back down south and pick cotton like you're supposed to, nigger?"

"Maybe we oughta ship your dirty black ass back to Africa in a box, Pickaninny. Huh? You like that nigger boy?"

"This is white man's country, nigger. Take your fuckin' shoeshine box back down to Alabama where you belong."

By this time Buckles, Diehl, Rengers, and Sabulsky have really started to boil, and Sabulsky yells "Hey! Hey! Come on you guys, knock it off. What the hell do you guys think you're doing?"

"Hey fellas, we got some goddamn nigger lovers down there. You sleep with that jungle bunny, white boys? You and that nigger big buddies are you?" The bleachers are getting into it more and more and showing support for their spokesman.

"Hey prick", Sabulsky hollers, pointing his finger right at the one with the biggest mouth, "shut your fucking mouth."

The guy stands up in the bleachers and says, "Why don't you come up and shut it for me, nigger lover?"

That did it. The four of them grab bats and started running toward the end of the ten foot high fence. Impulsive and admirable, but not very smart. When they reached Tugerson he corralled them with his arms and herded them back to the dugout. With the bleacher cowards still yelling in the background, Tugerson told his teammates to put the bats down and listen to him. He said, "Those guys out there are one of two things. They is right...or they is wrong. When they try to tell him he does not have to take crap like that he shushes them, and says, "Like I said, they is either right...or they is wrong. If they is right...and I am a dirty, no count nigger ought to be back in Africa or pickin' cotton somewhere...then they ain't doing nothing wrong. Can't fault a man for tellin' the truth. But if they is wrong...well then they gonna be judged by somebody a whole lot bigger than me or you all. Now sit down and relax, you guys...they ain't botherin' Big Jim."

The four that had grabbed the bats went back down the line and watched Tugerson finish warming up. They never let up on him, and he never changed expressions. Tugerson got his 28th win that night and broke Podres' record.

After the game, Tugerson referred to those in the bleachers as "little people," explaining, "They think they come out here and yell things at me make 'em feel big...you know, they can feel better than somebody. They got to feel important to themselves...they got to think they're better than they really are...'cause they is little and they really know that. They don't bother me, they really don't. 'Cause I know what they is and what I am. And so do they."

Winning, Grubb, and Winning

Steadily, through the months of July and August, the Smokies were winning, gaining ground in the race for second. Maryville-Alcoa had locked down first place and the pennant after the opening game of the season and had not let go. The race had been for second place, and in the end, the Smokies overtook Kingsport and assured a play-off series that started with the Morristown Red Sox, a team the Smokies knew they could beat. The Smokies knew it, and the Red Sox knew it.

Everyone knew that Tugerson would win two games, the first and one more. The Smokies just had to come up with someone to win game two. That someone turned out to be Ken Buckles. Tugerson won game one, allowing six hits and hitting a grand slam in a lop-sided 11-3 win. Buckles in game two played like Tugerson, allowing eight hits and knocking in five runs with as many hits for a more lop-sided win, 15-3. Morristown beat up Koehnke in game three, pounding him for sixteen runs with as many hits. Tugerson then won the series by winning game four. Next up, Maryville-Alcoa.

Game 1 against Maryville-Alcoa was reminiscent of a game played a month before against Big Stone Gap, only this time it was Maryville on the winning side of this 19-18 debacle. Everybody pitched but Tugerson, and Koehnke got the loss. Tugerson, as he had all year, picked them up again by winning Game 2 by a score of 5-4. Buckles started Game 3, but he just did not have it that day. Koehnke rose to the occasion in relief and redeemed his two other play-off losses with a 14-11 win. Tugerson again stepped up as he had time and time again, winning Game 4 and the series, 8-3.

The celebration on the field and in the locker room after Tugerson's 33rd win of the season was total, ultimate euphoria. Not even Grubb's financial antics could detract from what this team had accomplished. Although Grubb had initially promised $100 per man for the play-offs, he then reneged and threatened to pay nothing. In the end he paid $10 per man. All that was upsetting at the time but faded in time as insignificant compared to winning.

Winning. That's all that really mattered in the end. Looking back at all of it… the Parkway, Pennington Gap, Pankovits' signs, the joke on Sarracino, Bobby Grose, the unies being repossessed, Dick Carney, Harlan…all of it, made the Smokies a baseball team and winners. The thing that Buckles remembered most about the post-game atmosphere was no one could stop smiling—not Lindley, Griffith, Carney—not even Pankovits. It was wonderful. Wonderful because winning is always more fun when you are the only one who thinks you can do it, and wonderful because you care. The Smokies cared and they knew no one could beat Jim Tugerson when it really counted.

"And it didn't make a bit of difference whether it mattered one iota to anyone else whatsoever…it mattered to us. And we won. And it was special…and, at least for the moment, we were special, if only to each other."

Ken Buckles and Whitey Diehl

Chapter 12

The Recollections of Teammates Mobley and Clapp

Outfielder David "Pepsi" Mobley

David Mobley was the starting right fielder when Big Jim opened the Pankovits-managed Smokies against the Maryville-Alcoa Twins on April 25, 1953. Mobley was the first black player signed by Pankovits. He had gone to the plate twice for the Rock Hill Chiefs against the Smokies on August 26th of the previous year at Rock Hill in the Tri-State League. By opening in right field for the Smokies he broke the color barrier in two leagues in an eight-month time frame and had a good day doing it. Batting seventh in the order, he had two singles in five trips to the plate, scored a run, and played errorless ball. Mobley played in 22 games for the Smokies and finished with a .269 batting average. His best game was on May 1 in a losing effort to the Maryville-Alcoa club when batting in the three spot he had four hits in five at bats, scored a run, and drove in three.

I met David Mobley at age 83 at his Charlotte residence in late May 2008. Mobley spoke fondly of his baseball-playing days in his native Lancaster, South Carolina, at Rock Hill, at Knoxville, and later at Charlotte where he again played semi-pro ball as he had for the Lancaster Tigers. He was proud that he had been the first African American to play in the Tri-State League for the Rock Hill Chiefs against the Smokies in 1952, and that he was among the first black players to play for the Smokies in the Mountain States League in 1953. Mobley, like the Tugersons, was optioned to Knoxville by the Rock Hill Chiefs because of the reluctance of the Tri-State League, like the Cotton States League, to integrate. Also like the Tugersons, Mobley had played in the Negro leagues, having once donned the uniform of the Birmingham Black Barons. Mobley, like Buckles, Diehl, and Clapp, had great admiration and respect for Jim Tugerson. He admired not only Tugerson's pitching talent but his way of living as well. Mobley told me Tugerson wrote home often while in Knoxville and was "a family man."

Mobley shared a second-floor apartment with Jim, Leander, and Jim Brown, an infielder from the Raleigh area who was traded by the Smokies to Morristown, while in Knoxville. Mobley described the property I had already determined was located at 216 East Vine Avenue in Knoxville, an area that gave way to urban development in the form of the James White Parkway years ago. This was the address used by Syd Pollock, owner of the Clowns, to correspond with Schoolboy. In 1953 that property was owned by a Jessie Lee Freeman who operated Freeman Beauty Shop in the rear and rented out the top floor. Mobley recalled that they frequently ate at a couple of different restaurants in the vicinity that had great hamburgers, and that they ate plenty of them. These restaurants were subsequently identified as The Streak House and the Stream Line Café.

Mobley, the Tugersons, and Brown also stayed together in a house in Pennington Gap, Virginia when the Smokies were playing the Virginia and Kentucky teams. His memory, however, no longer stored any specific details of this home on the road.

Mobley reluctantly acknowledged that he was cut by the Smokies after his hit production decreased. He hit the ball well at the beginning of the season but later slipped into a batting slump from which he was unable to recover. After the Smokies won the Mountain States League Championship, he saw Tugerson pitch for a barnstorming team in an exhibition game in Charlotte. He talked to Tugerson after the game and shook his hand. (Mobley possibly may have confused this game with one played in 1951 involving the Jackie Robinson All-Star team as Charlotte was not on the schedule of the 1953 Campanella barnstorming team of which Tugerson was a member.) He has had no contact with anyone from the Smokies' team since then but knew that Tugerson had died several years ago.

David Mobley in August 1952

Smokies' Catcher David "Red" Clapp

Red Clapp was born and raised in the Corryton community of north Knox County and has lived his entire life there. When interviewed in March, 2008, he was 78, fit as a fiddle, and still working every day, cooking breakfast at the Sunrise Market & Deli. Clapp, retired from the State of Tennessee Public Service Commission, previously owned the Sunrise and continued to cook breakfast after he sold it. The name Sunrise seemed fitting since Tugerson cooked during the off-season at the Sunset Restaurant in Winter Haven before retiring from baseball.

Clapp played in the American Amateur Baseball Congress (AABC) World Series in Battle Creek, Michigan in 1946, 1947, and 1948. He played one game against the Cuban team that was managed by Fidel Castro. Bill Meyer signed him to a Pirates contract in 1950. He bounced around in the low minors and semi-pro ball and played for the Morristown Red Sox in the Mountain States League in 1952. He was playing for the Inskip team in the Knoxville City League when Dr. Grubb signed him on with the Smokies following an injury to the Smokies' regular catcher, Charlie Bradford.

Clapp and Pankovits never got along as Pankovits resented Dr. Grubb having signed him, a catcher. Clapp had a new mitt when he joined the Smokies and Tugerson wore it out in a month. Tugerson, barring none, was the fastest pitcher he ever caught. He recalled how Tugerson's fast ball backed batters off both sides of the plate. He blamed Pankovits for Tugerson not being signed by a major league team, alleging that Pankovits simply worked Tugerson too hard and wore him out. Clapp followed Tugerson's career in the Texas League and knew he never made it to the majors.

Clapp was proud that he was catching Tugerson at the end of the '53 season, a season he finished as the winningest pitcher in organized baseball. Clapp was also proud of his homer, triple, and two doubles that drove in eight runs the night Tugerson tied Johnny Podres' league record.

Clapp recalled Dr. Grubb paid him for all his playing time by giving his two daughters tonsillectomies, which were performed at the same time, in his office. His payment was to have also included $100 but Grubb never paid it.

David (Red) Clapp in 1958

Chapter 13

The Career After the Smokies

Following the Mountain States League championship series, Tugerson joined the Negro League Western All-Stars as a member of its pitching staff. Jack Aragon, Business Manager for the Maryville-Alcoa Twins that had just lost to Tugerson in the play-offs, arranged for a game between the All-Stars and the Indianapolis Clowns at Hunt Field in Alcoa on September 22, 1953. Of course, it was like old home week for Tugerson, who, along with this brother Leander, helped the Clowns win league championships in 1951 and 1952. A new member of the Clowns who was not on the team when Tugerson played there was Toni Stone, the first female professional baseball player. Stone played second base and batted .243 for the Clowns in 1953, her only year to be a Clown. Stone displaced veteran Clown second baseman Ray Neil, who moved to left field. The next year her contract was sold to the Kansas City Monarchs.

The Clowns beat the All-Stars at Alcoa that night, 4-0. Tugerson was relieved in the sixth inning due to cold weather. He gave up two hits and two runs in the six innings pitched.

Tugerson played with the Western All-Stars against the Clowns again on September 25th, this time at the site where he had been denied the opportunity to pitch just four months earlier—Hot Springs, Arkansas. Tugerson beat his old teammates 15-1 before 1,200 fans, and besides getting the win, he also hit a home run. Tugerson only pitched for the Western All-Stars during September.

In early October he joined Roy Campanella's Barnstorming team, the Tourists. Campanella had scheduled some 27 games in the southeast, southwest, west coast, and

Honolulu between October 9 and November 6, 1953. The other members of this team (besides Campanella and Tugerson) included Bill Bruton, Braves center fielder; Junior Gilliam, Dodgers second baseman; Harry (Suitcase) Simpson, Indians right fielder; Jim Pendleton, Braves shortstop; George Crowe, Braves first baseman; Don Newcombe, Dodgers pitcher; Joe Black, Dodgers pitcher; Connie Johnson, White Sox pitcher; Larry Doby, Indians third baseman; Dave Hoskins, Indians pitcher; Bob Boyd, White Sox left fielder; Othello Renfroe, Minot Mallards catcher; and Pat Scantlebury, Texarkana pitcher.

Tugerson made a return appearance at Alcoa with Campanella's team on October 10th against the Birmingham Black Barons and again won at Hunt Field 8-5 giving up six hits. This game was played in the afternoon so as not to conflict with the Maryville College-East Tennessee State College football game scheduled for that evening in Maryville. This barnstorming team had beaten the Black Barons twice the previous day in games played at Newport News and Richmond, Virginia. A paid crowd of 1,400 watched Tugerson pitch once again at Hunt Field, this time for Campanella's team, not the Smokies.

Tugerson remained with Campanella through at least the third week of October, traveling to Honolulu for three games October 19-21 against Eddie Lopat's All-Stars. Upon returning from Hawaii Campanella's team had several games scheduled in California but Tugerson is not believed to have stayed on the west coast for any of those games. His wife, Ora Lee, celebrated her 26th birthday while he was in Honolulu and was eight months pregnant with their last child. His devotion to his wife and their support for one another would not allow him to remain with the team any longer. He returned home to take care of his wife and family.

Campanella All-Stars Arriving in Honolulu October 1953

L. to R. front, Roy & Ruthe Campanella, Jim Pendleton, Dr. J. B. Martin, Don Newcombe, Bobby Boyd, Larry Doby, Pat Scantlebury, Junior Gilliam, Joe Black

L. to R. back, Jim Tugerson, George Crowe, Dave Hoskins, Bill Bruton, Harry Simpson

During the course of conducting one of an unknown number of searches on the Internet for information, the sale of an autographed baseball that had sold a few months previously popped up on the monitor. In August 2007, a signed baseball bearing the signature of Jim Tugerson on the sweet spot (preceded with an "X") with Satchel Paige and Joe Black above his, and Dave Hoskins and Roy Campanella below his, sold at auction on the Internet for $1,044. All these players, except Tugerson, played in the major leagues. Two of them, Paige and Campanella, are in the Hall of Fame.

In early December Dick Burnett of the Texas Eagles in the Class AA Texas League purchased Tugerson's contract from the Bathers, a move based on the recommendation of Roy Campanella. What Tugerson had no way of knowing at the time was that he would remain with the Dallas organization for the rest of his career and be forced to retire from baseball six years later. Even so he relished still being a part of the game and having the opportunity to play with and develop friendships with Pat Scantlebury, Bill White, and Dave Hoskins.

Scantlebury, who also had barnstormed with Campanella, joined Tugerson on the Dallas Eagles for the 1954 season and was 13-9 with an ERA of 4.12. Tugerson, however, after winning his first game, struggled and was sent down to Artesia (New Mexico) of the Class C Longhorn League. In a little over a month, he had posted a 9 and 1 record and had pitched 44 consecutive shutout innings and was recalled to Dallas in late May. By late July he had compiled a 7-4 record but then hit a 6-game skid during which he got almost no bat support. He ended the 1954 season with a 9-14 record and an ERA of 3.98.

Tugerson returned to the Dallas Eagles in 1955 and remained there for the entire season. He ended the year with a 9-12 record and a respectable 3.19 ERA. The Eagles won the regular season pennant but lost in the first round of the play-offs. Included among Tugerson's teammates that year were Ozzie Virgil and Bill White. Virgil, the first Dominican to play major league baseball, was the first black player to play for the Detroit Tigers. Bill White played 14 years in the majors and broadcasted Yankees games for 17 years. He then served as president of the National League from 1989 to 1994, the first African-American to hold such a high position in sports.

In mid-June 2008 Bill White shared his remembrances of Tugerson. White was in his third year of professional baseball in 1955. He was 20 years old and

Tugerson was several years older. He did not know how much older; they never discussed his age. Tugerson was his only black teammate. They roomed together on the road and shared a house in Dallas. Tugerson was like a father figure to White, and his wife, Ora, was very much a mother figure.

White acknowledged that he had a difficult time dealing with the racial slurs and bigoted remarks of the fans. Tugerson, being older and from the South, had a much greater tolerance of the verbal abuse than White. There were times when White got so upset that he wanted to grab a bat and go after those guys in the stands. Once when he threatened to do just that, Tugerson grabbed him, wrapped his arms around him, and said, "Hey kid, you can't do that. Things will get better." Tugerson had a calming effect on White.

Tugerson had a great influence on White that year, and he visited Tugerson at his home in Winter Haven several years later while in spring training at St. Petersburg with the Cardinals. Tugerson was a Winter Haven Police officer then, of course, and had been hired because he had such influence and was so visible in his community.

Tugerson played winter ball in Panama following the 1955 season but returned to Dallas for the 1956 season. After a May 18th start in which he failed to retire a hitter, Tugerson was optioned to Amarillo of the Class A Western League where he remained for rest of the season. He finished the year at Amarillo at 11-6 and an ERA of 5.67. He again pitched winter ball in Panama, but not for long. In November 1956, Tugerson became the second black police officer hired by the Winter Haven Police Department. He announced his retirement from baseball.

1955 Dallas Eagles Starting Four
Joe Kotrany, Stan Milankovich, Red Murff, Jim Tugerson

Tugerson remained in his police cruiser until the spring of 1958 when the department granted him another leave of absence so he could take one last shot at the major leagues. He returned to the Dallas Rangers and became a part of a pitching trio that punctuated The Rangers' last year in the Texas League. "The Big Three," as they were called in the Dallas paper, included Joe Kotrany, who was named Texas League pitcher of the year and led the league in wins (19-10); Dave Hoskins, Tugerson's buddy from the barnstorming days four years before who had returned to the minors, was 17-8; and Tugerson, who led the league in strikeouts with 199 and posted a 14-13 mark and an ERA of 3.33. Upon his return to Florence Villa following his stellar performance during the 1958 season, Schoolboy was honored by the City of Winter Haven with a parade and baseball game. The ceremony was presided over by Chief of Police Munsey Smith.

Tugerson at Lower Right

In 1959 Tugerson, granted another leave of absence from his budding law enforcement career, returned to Dallas, which was now in the American Association. At 36, he was a step away from the show, but did not have the kind of season he needed to get him there, posting a 5-12 record and an ERA of 3.51. After the 1959 season, Dallas re-assigned his contract to Sioux City, and although reacquired by Dallas, Tugerson decided to hang up his cleats for good and return home to Florida.

Beginning at age 28, Big Jim had played eight years of organized professional baseball during a nine year period. He had rubbed shoulders and played with Hank Aaron, Willie Kirkland, Roy Campanella, Satchel Paige, Joe Black, Dave Hoskins, Ozzie Virgil, Bill White, and others, including his brother, Leander. He had been the winningest pitcher in organized baseball in 1953 with 29 regular season wins and had broken a record set by Johnny Podres in doing it. He had led the 1953 Class D Knoxville Smokies to a level

114

only his teammates thought possible, and they had honored him by hoisting him upon their shoulders. He had, in deference to the furtherance of his own career, filed a landmark lawsuit because he had been denied his right to play baseball, an action that may well have been a greater nemesis to his career than Willie Kirkland presented to his success in the Mountain States League. Baseball would always be his first love, but the time had come for him to use those talents that had made him a leader in baseball in another career.

Chapter 14

The Life Before and After Baseball

James Clarence Tugerson was born March 7, 1923, in Florence Villa, Florida, and died April 7, 1983, in Florence Villa, Florida. In between he played baseball for at least 20 years, eight of them outside of Florida. He pitched for teams in Indianapolis, Oriente, Knoxville, Dallas, Artesia, Panama, and Amarillo. He barnstormed throughout the southeast and Hawaii. Before he left, he was a son to Beulah and Edward Tugerson, a brother to Leander, and a husband to Ora Lee Collins, whom he married June 9, 1946, almost four months after being honorably discharged from the United States Army.

After being inducted January 26, 1943, he entered into military service on February 2, 1943, at Camp Blanding, Florida, and was discharged February 18, 1946, at Camp Blanding. His MOS (Military Occupational Specialty) was Military Policeman, training and experience that would serve him well in his future life. The highest rank he attained was that of Corporal, and he was discharged a Private First Class. He served at Buckley Field in Colorado and was assigned to the 3702nd Army Air Force. His military enlistment, report of separation, and discharge record indicates he had a sixth grade education. His military record also indicates Tugerson received the ATO (Asian Theatre of Operations) Medal, the Good Conduct Medal, and the World War II Victory Medal.

Jim and Ora Lee had six children—Beverly, Barbara, Aundra, Letitia (Tina), James, Jr., and Gerald (Jerry). Before leaving Florence Villa in 1951 to play professional baseball, he worked as a short order cook at the Sundown Restaurant, a job he would return to during the off seasons. Florence Villa was, and still is, the predominantly black community in Winter Haven. It was Schoolboy's community. It was where he grew up, where he always returned during the off-seasons, where he raised his family, where he became a much respected community leader and police officer, and where he lived out his life.

Winter Haven Police Department 1962

Schoolboy at Upper Left

In November 1956, following his third season in the Texas League with the Dallas Eagles, Tugerson became the second black police officer on the force of the Winter Haven Police Department. He remained a Winter Haven police officer until his death on April 7, 1983. The City of Winter Haven granted Tugerson leaves of absences that allowed him to play his last two seasons of baseball with Dallas in 1958 and 1959. The City of Winter Haven also renamed the Avenue T Softball Field where Tugerson died as Tugerson Field. The field was dedicated in his memory on July 14,

1983, and a softball game between employees of *The News Chief*, Winter Haven's daily newspaper, and employees of the City of Winter Haven followed the ceremony.

Information relative to Tugerson's career as a Winter Haven police officer came primarily from five sources—J. J. Stanton, Coordinator of Personnel Selection & Recruitment, who worked for and with Tugerson as a rookie cop; Deputy Chief Edgar C. "Buddy" Waters, a patrolman working for Tugerson at the time of his death and a pallbearer at his funeral; and Lieutenant Joel Bennett, a sergeant under Tugerson, also a pallbearer; Tina, his daughter; and Tugerson himself. Stanton, Waters, and Bennett, all white, called Tugerson "Schoolboy" and "Schoolie" as his family and friends did. In time, they also came to affectionately call him "old man." Interestingly, neither Waters nor Bennett were familiar with Tugerson's baseball career, and Stanton only learned of it at the funeral when he observed memorabilia that had been put on display by Ora Lee. Schoolboy commented to Stanton once without explanation that he "had gone as far as he could go" in his vocation outside of Winter Haven, and had returned to work and be with his family. These men knew Tugerson as a police officer, not a baseball player, but they had the same level of respect for him that Tugerson's teammates had demonstrated.

Tugerson was a Shift Lieutenant during the time these officers worked with him. Both Stanton and Bennett joined the force in 1972 and worked with Schoolboy until his death. Bennett was Tugerson's sergeant, and Waters had been a patrolman under Tugerson for four years.

Stanton was a rookie officer from up-state New York in 1973 when he got a call from his mother telling him that his father was gravely ill and that he should come home. It was a Friday night, and he did not have enough cash to make the trip or any way to get it. In those days there were no ATMs, credit cards, or debit cards allowing you immediate access to cash. You had to try to cash a check, and there was always a limit on the amount. Schoolboy heard of his situation, came to him, and loaned him $300 to make the trip, telling him to repay the money when he could. He made the trip, but his father died before he got there.

Tugerson was a compassionate cop, but he was also very tough. He was street savvy and always demanded and got respect. He was "The Law" in Florence Villa, Winter Haven's black community. There were a number of shootings in the First Street area in the 1970's, and Tugerson was always the one to handle such calls. He could usually handle them without having to muscle anyone. Stanton recalled responding to a shooting on one occasion when Schoolboy got there at the same time. As Stanton was getting out of his car with his shotgun, Tugerson told him to put it down, that "these are my people, I'll handle it." And he did.

Schoolboy was always the officer you wanted as your backup. He could be physical if he had to be and was very convincing. His size was usually enough to dissuade a suspect or prisoner from fighting but not always. Stanton recalled Tugerson arriving at an arrest scene once when Stanton was trying to get a good size black man into the rear of his cruiser. The suspect was resisting and Stanton was hitting him in his mid-section with the end of his night stick, trying to double him up enough to push him into the back seat. When Schoolboy showed up he made a comment about how his patrolman (Stanton) was getting whipped, and he did not like what he was seeing. The suspect, who did not know Schoolboy, made a smart remark and made the mistake of calling him "nigger." Tugerson opened the other rear door of Stanton's cruiser and motioned for Stanton to hit him in the mid-section one more time. When he did Tugerson reached through the back seat, grabbed the prisoner by the fat of his jaws, pulled him through the back seat, and slammed the door on his head. Resisting arrest was over.

Bennett and Waters both related stories about how Schoolboy had physically backed them up. Tugerson's support on more than one occasion had spared Bennett, a man of short stature and slight build, physical beatings. He felt that Schoolboy had actually saved his life on two occasions. Waters echoed Bennett's claims.

When asked if they had ever heard the story of Tugerson responding to a shotgun homicide without his sidearm and arresting the shooter, all three laughed simultaneously and pointed out that Schoolboy never carried a weapon that you could see. The department issued a Colt Python .357 magnum, a real hog of a gun that Schoolboy refused to carry. Instead, he carried a .38 caliber Smith & Wesson model 37 5-shot revolver. He also refused to wear a police belt with holster, radio carrier, etc. Instead, he always wore a brown belt and brown shoes which drove the administration crazy. He carried his police radio in his back pocket. The administration complained but never took any action. Schoolboy was too valuable, too effective to alienate.

Tugerson was always doing things to make the officers around him better, tougher. Once about 3:00 a.m. Waters bumped into Schoolboy at the station, and Tugerson reached out his hand to shake hands. When Waters clasped his hand, Schoolboy swung him over a table and pinned him against the wall. Waters tried to come off the wall to fight, which he knew "was a bad idea," but he couldn't move. Schoolboy told him he had better know the man whose hand he is about to shake before he reaches his out.

Schoolboy was a habitual whistler and singer. He could be heard coming down the hall doing one or the other, and everyone knew who it was before he arrived. Once when he arrived after singing all the way down the hall, Waters gave him a look and Schoolboy asked, "What you looking at, Boy?" Waters asked him what he had done with all that money his mama had given him. Schoolboy asked, "What money?" Waters replied, "That money your mama paid for singing lessons." It was always fun "to get one on Schoolboy" because it was such a rarity.

Besides being an equalizer, a trusted backup, and a mediator in the black community, he also was an ambassador for the department. These officers named four black officers Schoolboy recruited, including Gay Henry, the lieutenant in charge of detectives, now retired. He was unofficially given the responsibility of recruiting black officers because he simply was better at it than any white officer could ever have been.

For several years Schoolboy was only allowed to arrest black suspects. The reverse of this was also true—only white officers arrested white suspects. This made the arrests less confrontational. Black suspects did not like being arrested by white cops, and white suspects did not like being arrested by black officers. Of course, the force was then and still is predominantly white.

Tugerson spoke of his law enforcement career in *The Ledger* interview. "When I was hired by the city, we were restricted to arresting black only. Couldn't arrest whites. Couldn't stop 'em. We had to strictly work the black neighborhood. We worked the Villa and went anywhere else where there were blacks." After 10 years Tugerson was promoted to sergeant but "...was a sergeant without authority. I was a sergeant over my own self." He got his next promotion three months after the department got a new chief. Tugerson was promoted to shift lieutenant and remained that rank until his death.

Bennett recalled being overwhelmed by the turnout at Schoolboy's funeral. He had no idea that Tugerson had touched so many lives in the community. Of course, Tugerson was a very private person and kept a lot to himself. Bennett had no knowledge of Tugerson's baseball career, but knowing about it now clarifies a lot of things he did not understand about him when he was alive. Bennett is a baseball fan, but he recalled thinking that Tugerson was goofing off because he either did not want to work or was taking advantage of his lieutenant's position because of all the time he spent every year at the Boston Red Sox spring training camp. Bennett understands now that Tugerson was simply drawn to the game. He could not stay away.

A number of people remember the night that Big Jim died, and three remember very vividly where they were and what they were doing. Deputy Chief Waters, who was a patrolman under Lieutenant Tugerson, was a couple of hours into his shift pulling a detail downtown he did not particularly like. The detail was one that Schoolboy had asked for volunteers at roll call, and after several moments, another officer finally volunteered to do. Waters commented that he wished he had spoken up sooner, joking that he really wanted to pull that duty. Schoolboy said, "You got it." Trying to be funny, he ended up getting what he did not want. Schoolboy got the last laugh.

When he heard the call on the radio, a black woman saying," Breaker! Breaker! Mr. Tugerson's down! Mr. Tugerson needs help!" He knew instinctively where Schoolboy was without the caller giving a location. He was closer to that location because of the detail Schoolboy had "volunteered" him to take. Waters left the downtown detail and drove to the ball field on Avenue T and 9th Street, which was not only a ball field but a popular gathering place for neighborhood kids. Schoolboy was on the ground and an EMT he knew, Frank Brown, was giving him CPR and had started chest compressions. Schoolboy looked at him with a look on his face that said, "Do something, Boy!" Waters took over the chest compressions from the EMT, but he knew it was no use. Tugerson had suffered a massive heart attack, and he died at the scene. There had been no game going on, but there were people milling around. Schoolboy had just stopped by the field.

His daughter, Tina, was at home fixing her dad a spaghetti supper and was waiting for him to come by and eat.

She heard a knock at the door. A police officer was standing there and told her that her dad had had a heart attack at the ball field, and that he was there to take her to the hospital. He was, of course, already dead when she got there.

Tina's son, James, who thought the sun rose and set on his granddaddy, and who had insisted on taking his granddaddy's name, was in Tallahassee with his grandmother visiting his aunt Barbara who lived there at the time. James can still hear that phone ringing and learning of his granddaddy's death. He was nine years old.

Lieutenant Jim C. (Schoolboy) Tugerson died on April 7, 1983, but wasn't buried until a week later. This was because a nephew, who was in the military and stationed in Germany, pleaded with the family to wait for him to get home. This nephew considered Jim his father. Normally, the military would not grant leave for a soldier to attend an uncle's funeral, but according to Tina, the Chaplain "twisted the papers," and the nephew was finally granted leave. During that week, her dad's body was in his casket at home, and there was a police guard with it 24 hours a day. Several family members, especially the younger ones, refused to stay at the house overnight.

Paul Johnson - The Ledger

Police pallbearers

"I know what he went through . . . Many of you cannot imagine what it was like to be a black police officer 28 years ago," former Mayor Lem Geathers told about 600 mourners at Thursday's funeral for Winter Haven police Lt. Jim "Schoolboy" Tugerson. Gay Henry, the lieutenant in charge of detectives, said Tugerson recruited him in 1969 and showed his greatness not only as a fatherly example, but in the good way he tou-

ched other lives. Tugerson, an avid Little League supporter, died of a heart attack at a city ballfield last Thursday evening. Family members attending the funeral included his widow Ora, mother Beulah Jones and six children. After a wake at the Tugerson home Wednesday, Thursday's funeral was at the Polk Community College gymnasium, followed by burial at Lakeside Memorial Park.

April 14, 1983

125

The service, in anticipation of a large turnout, was held in the Polk Community College gymnasium and burial followed in Lakeside Memorial Park, both in Winter Haven. Estimates of the number of people attending the funeral ranged from 600 to 1,000. The pallbearers included his sergeant, Joel Bennett, and seven patrolmen, including Edgar C. "Buddy" Waters. This police funeral included not only the members of the Winter Haven Police Department but law enforcement officers from all over Polk County. He was eulogized by former mayor Lem Geathers and Lieutenant Gay Henry, who had been recruited by Tugerson in 1969.

Following the death of her mother, Ora Lee, who died on her 73rd birthday October 19, 2000, Tina became the matriarch of the Tugerson family. She still lives in the house her dad bought and had trucked in two pieces to the lot he owned, with her two brothers, James, Jr., who drives a taxi in Winter Haven, and Gerald (Jerry), who suffered a severe stroke in June 2007 and is disabled.

Her dad had done some work on the house for the man who previously owned it and had commented to the owner at the time how much he thought his wife would like the house. Some time later the owner contacted her dad and told him he had a buyer for the property, which had been zoned commercial, and that the house was available. Her dad bought the house, moved it to the lot in two pieces, and put it back together.

That was 43 years ago—1965—when she was eleven years old. That same year, her uncle Leander, at age 37, died at his home near Gainesville, Florida, when he hit an electrical wire while adjusting his television antenna on his house and was electrocuted.

During the time her dad was playing baseball, the family went to Texas for six weeks during each summer. She recalled visiting with Bill White and his family, relating that they got to know the Whites better than any other ball players or their families. The trip to Texas was an annual event. They never traveled to Tennessee.

Winter Haven Hawks Early 1960's

Schoolboy at Upper Left

Schoolboy didn't give up baseball entirely following his retirement from organized baseball in 1959. He played for the Winter Haven Hawks, an all black team in the local league, in the early 1960's. He was also involved with youth baseball and managed a women's softball team at the field which now bears his name. Tina recalled her dad spent a lot of time at that ball park.

Schoolboy managed the women's fast-pitch softball team, the Trojannettes, for almost 25 years. The team, made up of women in their thirties and forties from Florence Villa, played an 18-game schedule in the Winter Haven city league. The team was also a traveling team and played other women's teams in Lakeland, Fort Lauderdale, and in other cities in central and south central Florida. Schoolboy was assisted by Ben Neal and Ruben Williams, manager of the Winter Haven recreation department. One of the players, Lily "Gussie" Jackson, who started out as a center fielder but was converted by Schoolboy to a pitcher, played until she was 49 years old. The team was practicing the night Schoolboy died. He had stopped by the field to see how things were going.

During the time her dad was a police officer, he would come home to watch a baseball game on television, parking the police car in front of the house with the radio on. Her assignment, from the time she was eleven until she was eighteen, was to monitor the radio and let him know if they were calling him. This required her to sit on the front steps rather than be out playing or doing something she wanted to do. His car number was either 54 or 57, and when she heard his number, she would take off running through the house telling him to come. He would tear out and make like he was somewhere else and seemed to be able to always respond in time to cover himself. Tina acknowledged that the department had to know what he was doing.

Another little known fact is that her dad was color blind. She always had to match his socks for him to make sure he did not leave the house with one blue and one brown.

Tina and the family still have and treasure her dad's baseball memorabilia—photographs, letters, newspaper clippings, and other items from the Indianapolis Clowns, the Knoxville Smokies, the Campanella barnstorming teams, the Dallas Eagles, the Dallas Rangers, and, of course, copies of the lawsuit filed in Hot Springs, Arkansas. Tina and her family realize more and more every day what all this meant to Big Jim—ball player, dad, granddaddy, and police officer, and to them.

Schoolboy at Home 1981

Chapter 15

The Best Shots Fell Just Short—
Fair Or Not

Roy Campanella was Schoolboy's trusted advisor and friend. He arranged for Tugerson to try out at the Dodgers' spring training camp at Vero Beach, Florida in 1952. The Dodgers of course, were interested but were not willing to pay the price demanded by Clowns' owner Syd Pollock. Pollock was a businessman and was in the baseball business to make money. And Tugerson was money. Based on Sam Jethroe's recommendation the Braves also wanted to take a look at Tugerson but this was after the Dodgers' try-out and Pollock's refusal to negotiate, so Schoolboy said no to the Braves.

The following year Campanella was encouraging Tugerson to make the move to organized baseball while Pollock at the same time was urging him to return to the Clowns. [Among the most haunting documents that Tina Tugerson had spread out before me on her dining room table was her dad's original 1953 contract with the Clowns dated January 22, 1953 and signed by both Pollock and Tugerson but obviously never returned.] Pollock had offered to pay Tugerson $350 monthly for the period May 15 to September 7, 1953. Schoolboy signed a contract with the Bathers for $100 less per month two weeks later. He made the very difficult decision to take less money for the opportunity to move up the organized baseball ladder. The National Association of Professional Baseball League on March 27th notified the Bathers of its approval of this contract. [Perhaps the most daunting document Tina Tugerson displayed was a letter dated April 4, 1953 to Jim from Syd Pollock.] Pollock wrote, "Wish you and Leander all the luck in the world in the Cotton States League...and you'll need plenty for as I previously advised the going is bound to be rough in those Mississippi towns."

In a second letter dated August 28, 1953 Pollock furnished Tugerson with the Clowns' schedule for eleven games between September 8th and 23rd which, according to Pollock, Tugerson should have been able to make following Knoxville's play-off games. Tugerson did, in fact, play two games against the Clowns as a member of the Negro League Western All-Stars at Alcoa on September 22nd and at Hot Springs, on September 25th prior to joining Campanella's barnstorming tour.

After the tour was over, Campy recommended Schoolboy to Dick Burnett, owner of the Dallas Eagles, and Burnett bought Tugerson's contract with the Bathers and brought an end to the civil action that had been pending in the Hot Springs' federal court for six months. Campanella knew that Schoolboy was the real deal. Tugerson's Knoxville teammates and fans knew he was the real deal. So did Willie Kirkland and Muscle Shoals. But Campy knew better than anyone else because he was a catcher. He caught major league pitchers for a living—a living he could not compromise by making an ill-advised recommendation. Campanella knew. The ability recognized by Campanella was not, of course, the only factor to be considered in advancing to the major leagues.

During the broadcast of the 2008 Civil Rights Game between the Chicago White Sox and the New York Mets from Memphis, ESPN commentator and Hall of Famer Joe Morgan spoke of lunch conversations he had with Happy Chandler, former Commissioner of Baseball and Governor of Kentucky, about Jackie Robinson. Chandler once related to Morgan a conversation he had had with Branch Rickey, the Brooklyn Dodgers' General Manager who signed Robinson to play with the Dodgers' AAA club, the Montreal Royals, in 1945. Rickey told Robinson that he would have to take "the high road" if he were to make it in major league baseball. Rickey made Robinson promise not to say anything, not to make any response, for the first two years regardless how bad it might get, regardless how humiliating, degrading, or belittling the environment might become.

Even though Jim Tugerson barnstormed with Jackie Robinson's team in the late 1940's, this advice apparently was never shared with him. If it was, the advice went unheeded. Rickey chose Robinson to integrate major league baseball, not because he was the best ball player around, but because he had the qualities necessary to endure what Rickey knew he would face from the baseball community, the fans, opposing players, and teammates. Chandler supported Rickey's signing of Robinson, but not everyone in baseball did. When Robinson started that game in April 1947 at Ebbets Field in Brooklyn against the Boston Braves, baseball and all professional sports changed forever.

Unfortunately, Tugerson apparently did not have the support of Branch Rickey, who, in 1953, was General Manager of the Pittsburgh Pirates. Tugerson was scouted by then Pirates' scout and former Pirates' manager, Knoxville native Billy Meyer, but no contract offer was ever extended. The first report of Meyer scouting Tugerson came on July 22, 1953, nine days after the lawsuit was filed in Hot Springs. Eleven days after this report, Joe Sewell, an Indians' scout was in Knoxville to see Tugerson pitch. Tugerson was at that time the winningest pitcher in organized baseball, and he finished the season the winningest pitcher in organized baseball. Was he simply not good enough to pitch in the major leagues? Or had an asterisk been put beside his name by major league owners and general managers who preferred to draw from a talent pool completely void of any controversy? Did he destroy his chances of playing in the major leagues by filing the lawsuit? Unfortunately, we'll never know the answers to these questions as the principals in this tangled maze have been cold in their graves for decades.

The one thing we do know for certain is that he was the winningest pitcher in organized baseball in 1953. He posted a record 29 wins in the regular season and 4 wins in the playoffs. He led the league in innings pitched, strikeouts, and shutouts. He broke the league record of 27 wins set by a 19-year-old Johnny Podres in 1951. This was good pitching, Class D or not, and maybe the best of his career.

Another certainty is that Tugerson was at his best when he was rested, was motivated, or was challenged. When any of these conditions existed during the 1953 season, Schoolboy's strikeouts, innings pitched, and shutouts would climb while his bases on balls, hits allowed, and ERA would decline. The Class D Mountain States League was clearly not worthy of his talent.

Unquestionably, Tugerson was a workhorse, throwing an estimated 5,377 pitches with the Smokies. By comparison, in the major leagues in 1953, only Robin Roberts exceeded the 5,000-estimated-pitch season with 5,147. In fact, only Warren Spahn and Roberts, two of the biggest aces in the majors, exceeded the 4,800 mark during other years of the early 1950's; Spahn had 4,838 in 1951, and Roberts had 4,872 in 1954. Schoolboy's catcher during his last month with the Smokies, David "Red" Clapp, may have been on mark in his assessment that Tugerson was worn out by the end of the '53 season.

During his season with the Smokies Big Jim's fans and teammates alike were awestruck by his talent and character. His fans brought him gifts on "Jim Tugerson Night," and his teammates hung on while Schoolboy pulled them through one of the most memorable seasons they would ever have. He took the high road in several of the towns where the Smokies played, enduring racial slurs, personal degradation, and humiliation. He refused to acquiesce when he filed the law suit, and did so because he thought his being banned from playing baseball in the Cotton States League simply because of the color of his skin was unfair, and he had to respond.

The closest he ever got to the major leagues after the '53 season with the Smokies was in 1959 when the Dallas Rangers became a part of the AAA American Association, putting him one step away from the majors. By then, however, Schoolboy was 36 and his window of opportunity had closed. He retired from baseball and returned home to support his family and pursue his law enforcement career.

Baseball had given him a lot. He had roomed with Hank Aaron in 1952 when both were with the Indianapolis Clowns. He had barnstormed with Roy Campanella, Junior Gilliam, Suitcase Simpson, Don Newcombe, Joe Black, Larry Doby, Dave Hoskins, Bobby Boyd, and others.

Baseball also took its toll on Tugerson. It never gave back as much as he gave it. Unfortunately, that's the way it was, and apparently, the way it was meant to be.

Several factors adversely effected Schoolboy's opportunity to play major league baseball—his race, his age, his signing with a team in a non-integrated league, his lawsuit, and possibly his being overworked. Tugerson, like many other black ball players that played in the Negro Leagues, were simply born too soon. Time simply ran out. But they paved the way for the generation that followed.

Had the year been 1973 and not 1953, even at 30 years of age, Schoolboy would very likely have been a part of the beginning of the modern day era of the dominant closer. Even though he had a limited curve and change-up, he had the overpowering sidearm fastball and pitched well in relief. Major league baseball in 1953 had not recognized the need for the closer. The likes of Hall of Fame closers Rollie Fingers, Rich "Goose" Gossage, and Dennis Eckersley did not come along until the early 1970's.

Schoolboy's affection for baseball, however, never waivered as evidenced by the more than 20 years he played, his reluctance to retire, his managing the Trojannettes, his hanging out at the Red Sox training camp every spring, his watching games on television while his daughter monitored his police radio, and his dying on a ball field, named in his honor posthumously. He was one of those who would have played for nothing.

Tugerson Field

Looking Down Right Field Line Toward Home

Renovated 2008

Chapter 16

The Tribute

On July 11, 2008, over a half century after Big Jim had offered to split that fan-donated $75 championship game pot with his teammates, he and his Smokies teammates were at long last honored prior to the Tennessee Smokies game with the West Tennessee Diamond Jaxx at Smokies Park in Sevierville. Tribute was paid to Tugerson as the winningest pitcher in organized baseball with his 33 total wins; tribute was paid to his teammates for rallying behind him and beating a team only they knew they could beat to become the 1953 Mountain States League Champions. The team was recognized for two other reasons. The '53 team was the first integrated Smokies team; it also was the first Smokies team to play in Sevier County before the Smokies' move from Knoxville to Sevierville in the year 2000.

A crowd of 6,294 watched as vintage photographs of Tugerson and the 1953 Knoxville Smokies flashed one after another on the new huge video board in left field. The photographs were of players now dead or dying. Photographs of Big Jim, Leander, Pankovits, Buckles, Diehl, Sabulsky, and "Sweet Cakes" Isley, most of which had been resurrected from the Tugerson family's memorabilia and scrapbook that had been closely guarded since Schoolboy's death in 1983. Also flashed on the screen was the only known team photograph, a snapshot which had been secreted away in the Tugerson scrapbook that had been enhanced, enlarged, digitized and was now through the magic of modern-day technology being electronically projected on a big screen for everyone to see.

As the array of pictures was being shown, the Smokies PA announcer read the story of the Tugersons and that Smokies team to those in attendance, only a handful of who had ever heard any of it. The fans heard about Tugerson rooming with Aaron, barnstorming with Jackie Robinson and Roy Campanella, the lawsuit, and his finishing out his baseball career with Dallas. The video presentation showed Tugerson with the 1953 Campanella barnstorming team wearing a pitching jacket and kneeling in front of Don Newcombe. Shots of or relating to Tugerson were flashed between innings. Shots of him in his police uniform, of his funeral, and of Tugerson Field closed out the video presentation.

The crowd at the park was the third largest of the season. The most fans had come to see future Hall of Famer John Smoltz pitch in rehab for the Mississippi Braves on May 24th while the second place attendance mark belonged to those who came to see the July 3rd fireworks extravaganza following the game that night. Attendance had spiked for the July 11th game, not just because the Smokies' had nailed down first place in the North Division, but to honor Big Jim and his Smokies teammates.

Both *The Knoxville News-Sentinel* and *The Mountain Press*, the Sevierville daily newspaper, had run great centerpieces in their sports sections the day of the game. Nick Gates, who had covered the Smokies for *The News-Sentinel* for years and had been hired by former Sports Editor Tom Siler in 1970, quoted a portion of Siler's interview with Tugerson on July 6, 1953. As a result of the coverage fans had called the Smokies all during the day seeking more information. Cobey Hitchcock, the young sports writer for *The Mountain Press*, had done an equally admirable job covering the planned tribute and had used both photographs of Tugerson and the Smokies team in his centerpiece account.

Honoring old ball players and military veterans, as fans and as patriotic Americans, makes all of us feel good. More often than not, they are one in the same. That was the case with the Tugersons and most of their Smokies' teammates. The majority of Big Jim's teammates were, like him, veterans of World War II. We all want to keep that feeling for as long as possible because we lose more of these ball players and veterans with every day that passes.

The video presentation began with the 1952 Clowns photograph of Jim and Leander sitting in the dugout with Buster Haywood and Ray Neil. Next came the best-known photograph of the Tugersons in their Bathers' uniforms, followed by Jim in his Smokies uniform. This was followed by the Campanella barnstorming team photograph taken a few days before they departed for the Honolulu series with Eddie Lopat's team. The Smokies' PA announcer read a prepared text as the photographs appeared and disappeared—one after the other. While the barnstorming photograph remained on the screen the letter from Bill White dated June 17, 2008, was read. The text of this letter was as follows:

"Jim Tugerson was a good friend of mine, a former teammate and roommate. Jim and I got to know

each other well during Spring Training with New York Giant minor leaguers in Melbourne, Florida. In 1955 both Jim and I played for the Dallas Eagles in the Texas League. I did not want to go to Dallas after two years of experiencing the problems of most early black players. My first year I was the only black in the Carolina League and my second year I was the only black on the roster of the Sioux City Soos of the Western League.

Jim Tugerson helped me get through the tough times in 1955. We were both from Florida. He was twelve years older, had played in the Negro Leagues, and helped calm me when things got rough. As roommates we constantly talked baseball and I made use of his knowledge of what to expect from pitchers and also how to act off the field. His wife, Ora, visited in Dallas. Her visit made us both happy because we got good home cooked southern food and Ora also made sure we got home on time. She and Jim were like a mother and father to me.

Years later, when I was with the Cardinals, I visited Jim at his home in Winter Haven and witnessed the respect shown him as a police officer. Jim Tugerson had the ability and size to command the respect of everyone.

Jim Tugerson was an excellent pitcher, a fine gentleman and a good friend. I will always remember the times I spent as his teammate."

Immediately following White's letter being read, the PA announcer introduced Big Jim's daughter, Tina; his 33-year-old grandson, James Tugerson, Sr.; and his 4-year-old great grandson, James Tugerson, Jr. All three had traveled from Jacksonville, Florida together to be a part of this event, and the crowd gave them a very warm reception. Tina and

139

James acknowledged the crowd's response with waves, and the applause and cheers intensified.

Following the Tugerson's introduction, photographs of the 1953 Smokies team, Pankovits, Buckles, Diehl, Sabulsky, Isley, Mobley, and Clapp were displayed on the video board accompanied by descriptive comments about each. Clapp, Mobley, and Tugerson then took the field to throw the ceremonial first pitch. All three had donned new Smokies jerseys bearing their names and the number 53 on all three backs.

Each of the three had also been given new Smokies caps. The response of the crowd when they took the field was the kind of thing that makes for immediate goose bumps. James again waved to the adoring fans as if he had been doing it for years. It soon became obvious to everyone that James was waving for someone who was there only in spirit. When they left the field, the crowd stood and roared it's loudest.

Reminiscent of 55 years ago, Tugerson pitched to Clapp while Mobley stood in at the left side of plate as he had then. Mobley, a feisty 83-year-old hitter, had been cautioned not to swing by Smokies President Doug Kirchhofer who was on the field coordinating the event. Mobley cooperated but asked for one more opportunity which Kirchhofer granted. Tugerson gave him a good ball to hit but Mobley's bat missed its mark, and he was disappointed. He later joked that Tugerson had "tricked" him by throwing a curve ball. As they came off the field each was given an engraved baseball displayed in a commemorative glass display case.

Clapp, Mobley, and Tugerson had been furnished the new Smokies jerseys and caps in the suite of Smokies minority owner Justice Gary Wade just prior to making their way to the field. When Mobley put on his jersey his body immediately became more agile, his movements more fluid, and his demeanor more youthful. The transition was incredible. He rose from his seat and walked over to a table where Justice Wade had a souvenir Louisville Slugger displayed. Mobley picked up the bat and struck a perfect batting stance, posing as he had in 1953 as a 28-year-old slugger. Mobley, a die-hard Mets fan, would say later in the evening that his being a part of this tribute was better than the World Series.

James Tugerson also shared his thoughts and feelings. Being nine years old when his granddaddy died, his memories are blurred and limited. Through the tribute he learned many things he did not know about his granddaddy, and as a result some of his childhood memories are now starting to make sense. James was extremely appreciative for this tribute as it helped fill a void in his life that had been there for a long time.

Aside from the tribute participants and their families, others on hand to share the good feelings that this tribute permeated included John Watkins, a retired law professor from Fayetteville, Arkansas who had written a paper on Tugerson and his lawsuit for the Polk County (Florida) Historical Museum; Bob Gorman, head of reference at the Winthrop University Library in Rock Hill, South Carolina who had written a paper published in "The National Pastime" in 2001 titled "David Mobley and the Rock Hill Chiefs," in which he had dubbed Mobley "The Jackie Robinson of South Carolina;" and Cato Clowney, a Negro Leagues historian, lecturer, and community leader from Maryville, Tennessee.

All these people mentioned in connection with this tribute—Justice Wade, Doug Kirchhofer, the participants and their families, Watkins, Gorman, and Clowney—"got it." There were countless others, both in attendance and not in attendance, who got it as well.

As James Tugerson was making his way to the field for the beginning of the video presentation and the on field activities, a 70-year-old man grabbed his shoulder and told him he worked at Chapman Highway Park where his granddaddy played and on occasion sat beside him in the dugout. The same man told Tina Tugerson as she was leaving the field how appreciative he was that she had come to Tennessee for this tribute and thanked her for doing so.

When Tina, James, and little James checked in at Knoxville's McGee-Tyson Airport on Saturday morning to head back to Florida, the ticket agent recognized the name and immediately struck up a conversation, telling James that he had seen his granddaddy pitch in 1953. James, always laid back, polite, and attentive, listened to every word the man had to say. The Tugersons made their flight, but with no time to spare. The ticket agent got it, too. He did not want to let go. But then, no one did.

Author's Note

The initial quest that resulted in this story being told was simply to establish that Chapman Highway Park existed and that a talented black pitcher named Big Jim Tugerson awed fans in that park in 1953 with his amazing sidearm fastball. Even though I was only nine years old at the time, I had a vivid recollection of the ball park and Tugerson.

I was troubled by the fact I could find no one among my family, my wife's family, or among our friends who had any knowledge or recollection of the things I remembered. My wife's grandparents lived in Seymour in Sevier County only a short distance from the park, and all those relatives who passed on Sundays on the way to visit regularly rode past the outfield fence but saw nothing.

I set out to prove the existence of Chapman Highway Park, Jim Tugerson, and the 1953 Smokies. I ended up doing much more than I ever contemplated. At the beginning my two primary sources were the newspaper archives of the Knox County Library and the vast resources of the Internet. I accumulated a mountain of information very quickly and learned things about Jim Tugerson I never knew as a 9-year-old or in later years even though I tried to copy his pitching style until I was 15. The Internet allowed me to collect data at a rapid pace and locate people that otherwise would have taken months or years to find. The same day I "Googled" Ken Buckles, I talked to him on the phone over an hour and met him in person ten days later. The same day I found Ken I also found Art Sabulsky the same way.

Having had a 25-year career as a federal investigator, I was well versed on hearsay and knew the pitfalls of inaccurate information such as the inaccuracies often repeated as gospel on the Internet. I found several mistakes as I proceeded, but I ventured to make all words written accurate and factual.

Perhaps the most egregious error I found was Big Jim's Winter Haven nickname, Schoolboy, having been transferred by someone to Leander. That mistake has perpetuated itself in print and on the web over the years. Interestingly, only his teammates and police colleagues in Winter Haven called him Schoolboy, after Schoolboy Rowe, and "Schoolie." His Smokies' teammates never knew the nickname Schoolboy. Big Jim never told them about Schoolboy or his age.

This was to be a non-fiction work, not a novel. I interviewed criminal suspects for years that preferred fiction over facts. My job was to weed out the fiction and identify the facts. This is how I approached this project.

As I researched, the most intriguing facts that surfaced were the circumstances that caused my getting to see Big Jim pitch at all in 1953. First, the Knoxville City Council had to vote in favor of building a new stadium during 1953 and doing without baseball that summer. Byron Kitchens and his investors had to obtain a franchise to play in the Mountain States League and find a ball field they could upgrade to minor league standards. They found one only 12 miles from my house in Sevierville. My dad had to alter his restaurant operation to have time to take me to the games. And Jim Tugerson had to be denied the right to pitch for the Hot Springs Bathers in the non-integrated Cotton States League and be optioned to the Knoxville Smokies. Not all of these things occurred for the right reasons, but they happened. These happenings egged me on to continue researching and interviewing.

I'll never be able to thank Ken Buckles and the family of Jim Tugerson, in particular, his daughters, Letitia (Tina) Tugerson and Barbara Birdsong enough for all their help. Ken shared with me not only his thoughts, comments, and recollections, but writings he had penned over 30 years before in hopes of having them published. When my wife, Janene, and I visited Ken at his home in Iowa, we had copied pertinent newspaper clippings, box scores, etc., from January through June, 1953. When Ken handed me copies of all the clippings from July 1st through the play-offs, saving Janene and me hours and hours or tedious, laborious reviewing and copying, I knew this was something I was meant to do. Tina welcomed Janene and me into her home in Florence Villa, a home that Schoolboy had built for his family 43 years before. She and Barbara shared photographs, newspaper clippings, and their stores about their dad. Barbara furnished me her clipping of her dad's funeral from *The Ledger* for inclusion in this book.

Having made reference to the newspaper clippings, I should say that although the coverage was scant and at times, half-heartedly reported, I could not have resurrected the game details and box scores without the Knox County Public Library's microfilm of the 1953 issues of *The Knoxville Journal* and *The Knoxville News-Sentinel.*

I want to express my gratitude to three other members of that Smokies' team—David "Pepsi" Mobley, Robert "Whitey" Diehl, and David "Red" Clapp, for their stories and recollections. Thanks also to J. J. Stanton, Coordinator of Personnel Selection & Recruitment; Deputy Chief E. C. "Buddy" Waters; and Lieutenant Joel Bennett of the Winter Haven Police Department for their revealing accounts about Schoolboy.

I should also recognize the help of Tom Muir, Curator of the Polk County Historical Museum, Bartow, Florida, whose assistance cut short wasted time and effort.

Tom also put me in touch with John Watkins, the retired law professor from Arkansas who unselfishly shared the fruits of his research with me. I'll be forever grateful for his help and guidance.

Finally, I should recognize the Internet as a whole and two websites specifically. Time after time I was able to find good factual information at my fingertips at Wikipedia, the free encyclopedia, and at the website of The Society for American Baseball Research (SABR).

I must now express my gratitude to my wife, Janene, my biggest fan, my toughest critic, and my most able assistant and traveling companion. Without her I would never have reached the note I am now composing. Two others that I should mention in the same breath are my daughter, Abby Allen Fetter, who unselfishly edited this work twice and Bill White who wrote so eloquently of his friend "Tug."

Unfortunately, I was never able to locate any of the black baseball fans in Knoxville who rode buses to Chapman Highway Park in Seymour to see Big Jim pitch, or who took Tugerson a gift on "Jim Tugerson Night," but I did find Raleigh Wynn, Sr. Raleigh, born the same year as Schoolboy, drove to Chapman Highway Park several times to see Tugerson's sidearm fastball that drew admiring fans from all directions. A two-time All-American at Tennessee State in football, a high school coach, a former Knoxville City Councilman, and the current Athletic Director at predominantly black Knoxville College, Raleigh was awed by the same talent I had attempted to emulate as a youth.

Time and death have robbed us of the opportunity to know more, but I've learned much that I didn't know. I hope that sharing what I have learned will somehow enhance the knowledge and love of baseball for fans everywhere.

2005 Ford 500